Amazing Grace

Messages on the Grace of God as Manifested in the Soul's Salvation and Enrichment

by

George Whitefield Ridout, D. D.

First Fruits Press
Wilmore, Kentucky
c2015

Amazing Grace: Messages on the Grace of God as Manifested in the Soul's Salvation and Enrichment / by George Whitefield Ridout.

First Fruits Press, ©2015
Original Publishing Company, [pubdate]

ISBN: 9781621712497 (print), 9781621712503 (digital), 9781621712510 (kindle)

Digital version at http://place.asburyseminary.edu/firstfruitsheritagematerial/105/

Ridout, George W. (George Whitefield), 1870-1959.
    Amazing grace : messages on the grace of God as manifested in the soul's salvation and enrichment / by George Whitefield Ridout.
    146 pages ; 21 cm.
    Wilmore, Ky. : First Fruits Press, ©2015.
    Reprint. Previously published: Louisville, KY : Pentecostal Publishing Company, ©1923.
    ISBN: 9781621712497 (pbk.)
    1. Grace (Theology). I. Title.
BT761 .R5 2015   234

Cover design by Wesley Wilcox

asburyseminary.edu
800.2ASBURY
204 North Lexington Avenue
Wilmore, Kentucky 40390

First Fruits
THE ACADEMIC OPEN PRESS OF ASBURY SEMINARY

First Fruits Press
The Academic Open Press of Asbury Theological Seminary
204 N. Lexington Ave., Wilmore, KY 40390
859-858-2236
first.fruits@asburyseminary.edu
asbury.to/firstfruits

Amazing Grace

MESSAGES ON THE GRACE OF GOD AS MANIFESTED
IN THE SOUL'S SALVATION AND
ENRICHMENT

By
GEORGE WHITEFIELD RIDOUT, D.D.,
of Asbury College
Author of " The Cross and Flag "

Pentecostal Publishing Company
LOUISVILLE, KY.

Preface

I HAD a most singular experience once with the subject *Amazing Grace*. I hope I shall not be thought forward or lacking in modesty if I tell the story. I was riding in a train in the West, one day,—I think I was going through Kansas—when I was moved to write a short article on the subject: *Amazing Grace*. I cannot now recall what I said in that article. I sent it on to the New York *Christian Advocate,* and it was published. Some months afterwards I received a letter from a lady in Milan, Italy, telling of the way the Lord had blessed her through reading that article. The letter I kept, it reads as follows:

" May a stranger thank you for your living, inspired article in *The Christian Advocate.*

" For years I have known much of that ' amazing grace.' It has enabled me to sing my way through many a tunnel. Over and over, by the dying beds of my dearest ones, and even by their graves, it has filled me with the very joy of heaven. Loneliness, loss of property, exile from my own country and the friends of a life-time, the anxieties which come with motherhood, the temptations to worry about the future—in all these things it has been more than conqueror and my soul has winged

its flight above the clouds and exulted in the light
of His countenance. But for some weeks past, under strange and very trying conditions, I had gotten
into the dark, and had begun to cherish thoughts
and feelings which I knew could not be pleasing to
God, and yet which seemed to entangle me in a web
of fine-spun steel, in which I seemed to have little
heart to struggle or even pray—a veritable snare of
the enemy. Yesterday morning I was reading your
article aloud to a member of my family, when I
came to the verse from ' Gospel Power.' I was immediately carried back to an *old-fashioned* camp
meeting. I could see the flare of the oil lamps on
hundreds of faces, the rough platform, the straw
in and around the simple altar rail, and I stopped
in my reading to recall the old tune, not heard in
many, many years. It came back to me immediately—that music by no means classical or artistic,
but with a lilt, a holy charm, a thrill of hope and
victory in it, the vehicle—that homely tune—of
God's ' Promise of Love Triumphant.'

" I sung it over and over, went about my work
still singing it, for as I sang the grace of God again
flowed into my life, restoring my soul. To-day I
am again proving yet, as often of old:

> " ' *With Thee conversing we forget*
> *All time and toil and care.*
> *Labour is rest and pain is sweet,*
> *If Thou, my God, art there.*'

" You will pardon this long personal letter, I am
sure. It seems to me that no matter how useful
and honored and busy a Christian man may be, a
word of gratitude for help rendered cannot be un-

acceptable, for we so often sow in tears and never know here if someone has gathered food or sweetness where we toiled with weary feet. So I venture to thank you from my heart. The testimony itself is not confidential, but my name I would have you please consider as a confidence.

" Yours cordially,

" _____ _____."

The hymn *Amazing Grace* is a great favorite of mine and I have chosen it as the title of my book in which I aim to set forth some of the wonders of Grace and attempt to write upon some aspects of the deeper things of God.   G. W. R.

Asbury College, Wilmore, Kentucky.

Contents

I. AMAZING GRACE 11

II. WONDERS OF CONVERTING GRACE . 24

III. THE WONDERS OF FAITH AND PRAYER. 34

IV. SIN AND SALVATION 45

V. GOD'S SKIES ARE FULL OF PENTE-
COSTS 58

VI. DOUBLE PORTION OF THE SPIRIT . . 68

VII. "DEEPER YET!" 79

VIII. THE BEAUTY OF HOLINESS . . . 90

IX. SPIRITUAL EXPERIENCES . . . 99

X. PREACHING THE GOSPEL . . . 107

XI. THE NEW THEOLOGY AND THE OLD
TIME RELIGION 120

XII. PERFECT LOVE 130

XIII. IF I LOSE MY FAITH . . , . 139

I

AMAZING GRACE

Amazing grace! how sweet the sound,
That saved a wretch like me!
I once was lost, but now am found,
Was blind, but now I see.
'Twas grace that taught my heart to fear,
And grace my fears relieved;
How precious did that grace appear
The hour I first believed!

Through many dangers, toils, and snares
I have already come;
'Tis grace hath brought me safe thus far,
And grace will lead me home.
The Lord has promised good to me,
His word my hope secures;
He will my shield and portion be
As long as life endures.

A BRITISH writer has well said: " There are two supreme tests of any interpretation of the Cross; one is, does it issue in a life of active service to our fellow-men, which we owe as redeemed men and women? Has our doctrine an ethical impulse and control? The other test is: does it evoke adoring gratitude to God? Does it leave us ' lost in wonder, love and praise? ' "

Addison touched this note when he sang:

> " When all Thy mercies, O My God,
>   My rising soul surveys,
> Transported with the view, I'm lost
>   In wonder, love, and praise."

Then Charles Wesley echoed it.   His hymn of adoration runs out into the prayer:

> " Finish then Thy new creation;
>   Pure and spotless let us be;
> Let us see Thy great salvation,
>   Perfectly restored in Thee,
> Changed from glory into glory,
>   Till in heaven we take our place,
> Till we cast our crowns before Thee,
>   Lost in wonder, love, and praise."

When preaching in France, one Sabbath morning, my appointments took me out of Chaumont down through a lovely valley country and then through Clairvaux (beautiful valley) where in the long ago that man of God, Saint Bernard, lived and preached and prayed and sang his hymns of adoration and praise.

It is said of Bernard that he devoted himself to study and exposition of the Bible.   In the solitude of the woods and fields, in prayer and contemplation he sought communion with God.   The chief object of his contemplations was the being and perfections of God and in dwelling on these his soul rose to ecstasy, and often in preaching his impetuosity of spirit and his ardour bore all before him.

Once he said, " Who will give me before I die to
see the Church as it was in the ancient days; when
the apostles cast their nets to catch souls, not silver
and gold."

In one of these seasons of holy joy, Bernard
wrote:

> " Jesus, the very thought of Thee
> With sweetness fills my breast;
> But sweeter far Thy face to see,
> And in Thy presence rest.

> " Jesus, our only joy be Thou,
> As Thou our prize will be;
> Jesus, be Thou our glory now,
> And through eternity."

While in the South, I was struck with the unusually earnest way they sing the old hymn,
Amazing Grace. When all other singing would
drag, announce *Amazing Grace* and new life would
take hold of the congregation. I shall tell in this
chapter the story of Rev. John Newton who wrote
this wonderful hymn. He indeed had been, as he
describes it, a " wretch " of a sinner and transgressor. John Newton's mother had prayed from
his infancy that he might become a preacher of the
Gospel but she died without seeing her prayers answered. He had little schooling and at eleven years
of age he went to sea with his father with whom
he sailed six years. Then he joined the navy and
became a midshipman. He plunged into infidelity

and became a reckless sinner. He went from bad
to worse until finally he found himself in the
service of a slave-dealer and became a slave himself
to his brutal master.

Once in a drunken bout he fell into the sea. It
was night, the tide was running strong, and he was
in grave danger of drowning, but one of the sailors
caught him by the neck and he was dragged on the
deck.   Among the books aboard his ship was
Thomas Kempis' " Imitation of Christ."   The
reading of this book reminded him of his lost condition.   One night at the wheel his fast life rose
up before him and he was led to cry: " My
mother's God, the God of mercy, have mercy on
me."   After his conversion he left the sea and became a tide surveyor at Liverpool.   He became a
diligent student and obtained an excellent knowledge of Hebrew, Greek, and Latin and found in-
creasing delight in the Scriptures and felt a great
desire to preach the Gospel.   He says: " I thought
I was above most living, a fit person to proclaim
that faithful saying that Jesus Christ came into
the world to save the chief of sinners, and as my
life had been full of remarkable turns, I was in
hopes that sooner or later he might call me to his
service."   Eventually he became an ordained minister of the Established Church, John Wesley and
George Whitefield being two of his chief sponsors.
Besides the wonderful hymn *Amazing Grace,* John
Newton also wrote this charming hymn:

" How sweet the name of Jesus sounds
   In a believer's ear
 It soothes his sorrows, heals his wounds,
   And drives away his fear.

" Dear name! the Rock on which I build,
   My shield, and hiding place,
 My never failing treasury filled
   With boundless stores of grace!

" Jesus! my Shepherd, Brother, Friend,
   My Prophet, Priest and King;
 My Lord, my Life, my Way, my End,
   Accept the praise I bring.

" Weak is the effort of my heart,
   And cold my warmest thought,
 But when I see Thee as Thou art,
   I'll praise Thee as I ought.

" Till then I would thy love proclaim
   With every fleeting breath;
 And may the music of thy name
   Refresh my soul in death!

NEWTON'S RING DREAM

One of the most remarkable dreams on record is the following which Newton had when he was suffering conviction for sin. It sets forth the value of the soul in language most unusual and extraordinary. The dream Newton tells as follows:

" The dream is certain and the interpretation thereof sure. I am sure I dreamed to the following effect and I cannot doubt, from what I have seen since, that it had a direct and easy application to

my own circumstances, to the dangers in which I
was about to plunge myself and to the unmerited
deliverance and mercy which God would be pleased
to afford me in the time of my distress.

" The scene presented to my imagination was the
harbor of Venice, where we had lately been.   I
thought it was night, and my watch upon the deck;
and that as I was walking to and fro by myself, a
person came to me, and brought me a ring, with
an express charge to keep it, carefully; assuring
me, that while I preserved that ring I should be
happy and successful; but if I lost or parted with it,
I must expect nothing but trouble and misery.   I
accepted the present and the terms willingly, not in
the least doubting my own care to preserve it, and
highly satisfied to have my happiness in my own
keeping.   I was engaged in these thoughts, when a
second person came to me, and observing the ring
on my finger, took occasion to ask me some questions concerning it.   I readily told him its virtues;
and his answer expressed a surprise at my weakness, in expecting such effects from a ring.   I think
he reasoned with me some time upon the impossi-
bilities of the thing; and at length urged me, in
direct terms, to throw it away.   At first I was
shocked at the proposal; but his insinuations pre-
vailed.   I began to reason and doubt myself; and
at last plucked it off my finger, and dropped it over
the ship's side into the water; which it had not
sooner touched, than I saw, the same instant, a ter-

rible fire burst out from a range of mountains, which appeared at some distance behind the city of Venice. I saw the hills as distinct as if awake, and they were all in flames. I perceived, too late, my folly; and my tempter, with an air of insult, informed me, that all the mercy God had in reserve for me was comprised in the ring which I had wilfully thrown away.

" I understood that I must now go with him to the burning mountains, and that all the flames I saw were kindled upon my account. I trembled, and was in great agony; so it was surprising I did not then awake; but my dream continued; and when I thought myself upon the point of a constrained departure, and stood, self-condemned, without plea or hope, suddenly either a third person, or the same who had brought the ring at first, came to me, and demanded the cause of my grief. I told him the plain case, confessing that I had ruined myself wilfully, deserved no pity. He blamed my rashness, and asked if I should be wiser supposing I had the ring again? I could hardly answer this: for I thought it was gone beyond recall. I believe, indeed, I had not time to answer, before I saw this unexpected friend go down under the water, just in the spot where I had dropped it; and he soon returned, bringing the ring with him. The moment he came on board, the flames in the mountains were extinguished, and my seducer left me. Then was 'the prey taken from the hand of

the mighty, and the lawful captive delivered.' My
fears were at an end, and with joy and gratitude
I approached my kind deliverer to receive the ring
again; but he refused to return it, and spoke to this
effect: 'If you should be intrusted with the ring
again, you would very soon bring yourself into the
same distress: you are not able to keep it; but I will
preserve it for you and whenever it is needful, will
produce it in your behalf.'

"Upon this I awoke in a state of mind not easy
to be described: I could hardly eat, or sleep, or
transact my necessary business, for two or three
days. But the impression soon wore off, and in
time I totally forgot it; and I think it hardly occurred to my mind again till several years afterward. It will appear, in the course of these
papers, that a time came when I found myself in
circumstances very nearly resembling those sug-
gested by this extraordinary dream, when I stood
helpless upon the brink of an awful eternity; and
I doubt not that had the eyes of my mind been then
opened, I should have seen my grand enemy, who
had seduced me wilfully to renounce and cast away
my religious profession, and to involve myself in
most complicated crimes, pleased with my agonies,
and waiting for a permission to seize and bear my
soul away to his place of torment. I should, perhaps have seen likewise, that Jesus, whom I had
persecuted and defied, rebuking the adversary,
challenging me for His own, as a brand plucked

from the fire, and saying, 'Deliver him from going down to the pit: I have found a ransom.'

"However, though I saw not these things I found the benefit: I obtained mercy. The Lord answered for me in the day of my distress; and blessed be His name, He who restored the ring (or what was signified by it), vouchsafes to keep it. Oh what an unspeakable comfort is this, that I am not in my own keeping! 'The Lord is my Shepherd.' I have been enabled to trust my all in His hands; and I know in whom I have believed. Satan still desires me, that he may sift me as wheat, but my Saviour has prayed for me, that my faith may not fail. Here is my security, and power; a bulwark against which the gates of hell cannot prevail. But for this many a time and often (if possible) I should have ruined myself since my first deliverance; nay, I should fall, and stumble, and perish still, after all that the Lord has done for me, if His faithfulness were not engaged in my behalf, to be my sun and shield even unto death. 'Bless the Lord, O my soul.'"

Amazing Grace is seen in *God's pardoning love and power*. Well has Dr. Owen, the eminent preacher of olden times, written:

"If there be any pardon with God, it is such as becomes Him to give. When He pardons He will abundantly pardon. Go with your *half*-forgiveness, limited conditional pardons, with reserve and limitations, unto the sons of men: it may be, it may become them, it is like themselves. That of God is absolute and perfect, before which our sins are as a cloud before the east wind and the rising sun. Hence He is said to do this work with His *whole heart* and with His *whole soul*. . . . We are apt to think we *are very willing* to have forgiveness, but that *God is unwilling* to bestow it; and that because He seems to be a loser by it, and to forego the *glory of inflicting punishment* for our sins; which of all things we suppose He is most loath to part withal. And this is the very nature of *unbelief*. But indeed things are quite otherwise. He hath in this matter, through the Lord Christ, ordered all things in His dealings with sinners to *the praise of the glory of His grace*. His design in the whole mystery of the Gospel is to make His *grace glorious*, or to *exalt* pardoning mercy."

Amazing Grace, furthermore, is seen in the work of sanctification. John Fletcher has defined entire sanctification thus: " It is the depth of evangelical repentance, the full assurance of faith, and the pure love of God (and man) shed abroad in a faithful believer's heart by the Holy Ghost given unto him to cleanse him and to keep him clean from all the filthiness of flesh and spirit; to enable him to fulfill the law of Christ according to the talents he is entrusted with and the circumstances in which he is placed in this world."

Dr. Daniel Steele, who was the John Fletcher

of the Methodist Holiness Movement, tells of the exuberance of joy that was his when he entered this rich and deep experience of sanctification, after coming to see his need of it under the ministry of A. B. Earle, the Spirit-filled Baptist evangelist. Dr. Steele says: " But language is wholly inadequate to express a manifestation of Christ which did not formulate itself in words, but in the mighty, overwhelming pulsations of love. The joy for weeks was unspeakable. . . .

" The ecstasy has subsided into a delicious and unruffled peace, rising into ecstasy only in acts of especial devotion. I find no fear of man nor of death. I can no longer accuse myself of unbelief, the root of all sin. What may be in me, below the gaze of consciousness, I do not know. I must wait till occasions shall put me to the test. It would not be wise for me to assert that all sinful anger—there is a righteous anger—is taken away, till I have passed through a college rebellion, or something equally provoking.

" If sin consists only in active energies, I am not conscious of such dwelling within me. If sin consists in a state, as some assert, I infer that I am not in such a state, from the absence of sinful energies flowing therefrom, and more especially from the indwelling of the Holy Spirit. I have had no other direct witness than that attesting Christ's love to me

" My experience," he writes, after enjoying this

blessing several months, " of the joy of the Holy Ghost grows richer and richer. Every day I seek a place for secret praise. I am filled and flooded with a sense of the divine love. How delightful any kind of service for the blessed Master! How sweet to feel His circling arms around one on every side—so that no calamity can possibly befall the soul!"

One of the older divines, preaching on John 3:16, used the following divisions: (1) The Lake; (2) The River; (3) The Pitcher; (4) The Draught.

The Lake—God so loved the world;

The River—That he gave his only begotten Son;

The Pitcher—That whosoever believeth on him;

The Draught—Should have everlasting life.

The story is told of an untutored preacher from the backwoods somewhere who was being examined in the preacher's course of study of long ago. Among the questions asked him was, " Which is the biggest river in the country?" His reply was: " The River of Salvation." The fellow evidently had a better knowledge of spiritual geography than he did of the physical, because he had it right when touching salvation. Ezekiel saw this river and describes it in chapter forty-seven. He sees it rise till it reaches the ankles, the knees, then the loins, and it becomes a river to swim in; and thank God, wherever this river flows it brings cleansing and life and plenty.

Phoebe Palmer saw it when she sang:

> " Amazing grace ! 'tis heaven below
> To feel the blood applied ;
> And Jesus, only Jesus knows,
> My Jesus crucified."

Finally, Amazing Grace is dying grace. " Oh, those rays of glory!" said Mrs. Clarkson when dying. " My God, I come flying to thee!" said Lady Alice Lucy. Lady Hastings said, " Oh, the greatness of the glory that is revealed to me!" " Oh, sweet dying!" said Mrs. Talbot, of Reading. " If this be dying," said Lady Glenorchy, " it is the pleasantest thing imaginable." " Victory, victory, through the blood of the Lamb!" said Grace Bennett. " I shall go to my Father this night," said Lady Huntingdon. The dying injunction of the mother of the Wesleys was, " Children, when I am gone, sing a song of praise to God." " Though a pilgrim walking in the valley, the mountain-tops are gleaming from peak to peak," said Miss Florence A. Foster.

II

THE WONDERS OF CONVERTING GRACE

Sudden conversions—such an amazing revulsion, such a complete and total transformation of character is an achievement possible only to religious influence. Hypnotism as I know can undoubtedly cure some men of their vice, drugs are able in certain cases after a long and difficult treatment to remove the taste for alcohol, but it is only a religious force which in the twinkling of an eye can so alter the character of a man that he not only then and there stands utterly free from tyrannical passion but is filled full of a great enthusiasm.—HAROLD BEGBIE.

"REGENERATION," says Richard Watson, "is that mighty change in man wrought by the Holy Ghost, by which the dominion which sin has over him in his natural state, and which he deplores and struggles against in his present state, is broken and abolished; so that with full choice of will and the energy of right affection he serves God freely, and runs in the way of His commandments."

A great mystery is converting grace! Nicodemus, that master of Israel, as he heard about it could only say in his amazement, "How can these things be?" "The dynamics of the phenomenon (we call conversion) elude our philosophy," says

one writer. Coleridge, writing about it said, " By
what manner of working God changes a soul from
evil to good; how He impregnates the barren rock
with gems and gold is to the human mind an im-
penetrable mystery in all cases alike."

" It is only a religious force," says the eminent
English writer, Harold Begbie, " which in the
twinkling of an eye can so alter the character of a
man, that he not only there and then escapes and
stands utterly free from tyrannical passions, but is
filled full of great enthusiasm and desire to spend
his whole life in working for righteousness, and
feels as if he had fed on honey dew and drank the
milk of paradise."

Someone has put the points or stages culminat-
ing in conversion thus:

1. Perplexity and uneasiness.
2. Climax and turning point.
3. Relaxation marked by rest and joy.
4. Release of dormant powers.

We see all these illustrated in the conversion of
John Wesley. " I am clearly convinced," he said
to Peter Bohler, " of unbelief—of the want of that
faith whereby alone we are saved." " Lord, give
me," he prays, " a full reliance on the blood of
Christ shed for me, a trust in Him as my
Christ, as my sole justification, sanctification and
redemption."

" May 24, 1738, he goes that night to Aldersgate
Street Chapel and listens to a man reading Luther's

preface to the Epistle of Romans about quarter before nine. The speaker describes the change which God works in the heart through faith. Wesley's prayer for faith now becomes the breathing of faith. He feels his heart strangely warmed. Wesley rises and testifies thus: "I now for the first time feel in my heart that I trust in Christ, Christ alone, for salvation. I have an assurance that He has taken away my sins, even mine, and saved me from the law of sin and death."

Charles Wesley celebrates the joy of converting grace in the following lines:

"Long my imprisoned spirit lay,
    Fast bound in sin and nature's night;
Thine eye diffused a quickening ray,
    I woke, the dungeon flamed with light;
My chains fell off, my heart was free,
    I rose, went forth, and followed Thee.

"No condemnation now I dread;
    Jesus and all in Him is mine!
Alive in Him, my living Head,
    And clothed in righteousness divine;
Bold I approach the eternal throne,
    And claim the crown, through Christ my own."

I have before me, which I will insert here, the unique account of a sailor's conversion. He was a Norwegian and his prayer and testimony are in broken, almost distracted English, but the genuineness of the conversion will impress you. He prays as follows:

" ' Dear Fader Gott, you know I haf been so bat, zo fery bat. I haf been blag lige pitch. I tink bat, speak bat, do bat, all day, efery day. Unt den you make me know you lofe me; you make me see mineselluf yoost as I vas, but I benn afrait. But now I know, Glory to Gott! I know the blag sin is gone; I am all nice unt vite inside, unt I don't afrait any more.' Afterward Jem spoke in a public religious meeting in this style, and a more forcible, pointed, and effective style has never been employed by any doctor of divinity: 'Dear Vrients: You hav asked me to tell you vat de Lort haf done for me. How can I dis do? Ven I tink of His gootness unt lofe, I hav not vorts efen in mine own langridge to speak of it; how den can I tell you in Engelisch, vish I only talk like any oder sailor-man? But yet I not can say no. I vas a teufel—I dink vorse, because de teufels dey haf no hope, und I haf shut my soul up from hope myselluf. If dere is anything bad I can do, I haf do it. I haf hate de dear Vater Gott, I haf hate all His peoples. O, is dere anything bad I haf not do? I will say not any more aboud my sins, because I haf much shame for dem, unt yet I feel dat if I talk 'bout dem, I vill tink mooch of myselluf, pecause I haf been so bad. Unt more, I vas so misbul. I nefer haf no peace, I nefer haf no res', I nefer haf no pleasure, 'cept I ked tronk unt fight, unt dat cos' all de money I vork so hardt for. Den I come to Port Chalmers unt I go into de meetin', unt I hear a man say dat de Lort Jesus Christ is come to tell man vat Gott is; dat Gott ton't hate me, an' not vant me to die unt go to hell; dat hell ain'd vatin' for me, but Gott vaits alvus, unt dat He ben sorry dat I vas not happy. He tell me dat der is only von man can send me to hell, unt dat is me myselluf, unt dat if I come unt ket into His hants der ain't no von—no, not efen de Sattan himselluf —dat can pull me 'vay agen. Unt vile I lissen unt hear effery vort, beliefing id's all true—'pout somebody elles—I hear a vort in here [striking his breast] dellin' me, " Yes, Yem, you ben de man all dis for." Unt I don't vait anoder minit. I belief id. I say: " Yes, Lord Yesus, I ben de man you die fur. Unt now I ben coin' to gif myselluf all pop fur you." Unt, if any man say to me any more, " How do you know all dis? " I say to him, " How I knod? Vat you tink id is keep me frum svearin', frum bein' bucko, frum keddin' tronk, frum hatin' myselluf unt eferpody elas? You ton't know? Vell, I do. Id ben de Lort Gott Almighty. Nopotty ellas can do it." Unt now I vast yoost like a leedle shild. I haf lose de taste for de bad, unt find it for de goot, t'ank Gott. Unt if I, dot vas so bad, unt ton't know anything 't all, get holt of dis goot ting, who in de vorlt coin' to be left oud? Gott bless eferpody, for Yesus Christ's sake, Amen.' "

Cowper, the poet and author of " There is a fountain filled with blood," when first led to see

the black cloud of his sins, was guided by the Holy
Spirit into peace and joy by one day reading the
words of Romans 3:24, 25: "Being justified
freely by His grace through the redemption that is
in Christ Jesus whom God hath set forth to be a
propitiation through faith in His blood." He saw,
as he sat musing on the words, how God waits not
for merit in us but advances to us from motives of
love that spring up in His own bosom, and how He
meets what the law demands by the offering of
His own Son—an offering which is held forth for
the acceptance of every sinner that has a heart to
understand.

Colonel Gardiner, of the British Army, was a
desperate sinner. The mercy of God reached him
and he was in the throes of the most awful conviction for weeks—his gloom was almost past endur-
ance. In October, 1719, he read the words:
"Whom God hath set forth to be a propitiation
through faith in His blood, to declare His righteousness for the remission of sins that He might
be just and the Justifier of him that believeth in
Jesus" (Rom. 3:25, 26). Here he saw the riches
of redeeming grace and love in such a manner as
even swallowed up his whole heart in love; so that
for seven years after he had thus drunk of this
well, he enjoyed a heaven upon earth, from the
time of his waking in the morning till evening
closed his eyes.

The following account of the remarkable conversion of Jim Owen has been given by Dr. George W. Truett, of Texas:

" I'll tell you of the most marvelous conversion I ever saw. I have told you it was my joy every summer to preach in the cattle camps in West Texas. One year when I went some of the men came to me and said, ' There is one man here on whom you need not waste your time, and that is ex-Sheriff Jim Owen. He'll come once, then he'll curse you all over the mountains; he always does.' They described him to me so that I could not miss him. One evening I went to preach, and as I stood before that great congregation in came Jim Owen. I preached and the Spirit of God moved mightily over that great audience and many sinners came, but there Jim sat with a most intent gaze upon his face but apparently unmoved.

" After the service we stood around talking, and some said, ' Jim Owen was here tonight, but he'll never come again. He'll curse you out; he always does when any preacher comes. He'll come once and then curse you and the Church out,' but some of the others said, ' No, I believe he will be back; he had a peculiar expression on his face that he never had before; he'll come again.'

" I started for my lodging place, some rods from the camp, away from the noise, over a mountainous region, when I heard someone talking, but as I drew nearer I realised that there were two of them, and that they were praying. I did not mean to eavesdrop, but I was held to the spot. They prayed something like this, ' Oh, God, thou hast promised that if two of us shall agree on earth as touching anything that we shall ask, that thou will give it us. We are praying tonight for Jim Owen. They say he can't be saved, but Oh, God, thou canst save the vilest sinner. Save him and let the people know that nothing is too hard for God; save Jim Owen, that Thou mightest close the mouths of the people and get the glory to Thyself.' That's the way to pray, that's the way to pray.

" I slipped away—they never knew I heard their prayer—but I did not sleep. The next evening when I stood up to preach, in came Jim Owen. All the sermon that I had prepared fled, and I said, ' We'll sing a stanza and then I'll ask this brother in front to lead in prayer, asking that God will give me the right message. His Spirit knows the need of these hearts.' I preached that night from the parable of the Prodigal Son, telling it as simply as to a little child. I said: ' Here was a man well reared, but he abused it, good environment but he trampled it under foot and went away despite the protests of his father and friends and wasted his substance; but when he had spent all he came to himself. Oh, that men would come to themselves! He said, " I will arise and go to my father, and shall say unto him, father, I have sinned against heaven and in thy sight and am no more worthy to be called thy son; make me as one of thy hired servants." He not only made the good resolution, but he kept it; he arose and came. Now I see that old father at the gate; He's watching. "Oh, how I wish my boy would come home; how often have I longed for him! Who is this coming? It walks like my boy, but so many have passed that I thought walked like him, but as he draws nearer, he looks more like him," and when he was yet a great way off the watching father recognised him and ran and fell upon his neck and kissed him.

" 'If there is a man in this audience that is in this poor prodigal's condition, I've a friend for him. If there is such a man and he wants to come back let him come down the aisle and take my hand,' and Jim sprang to his feet and came, reeling like a drunken man because of the intensity of his emotions. Everyone was on his feet in a moment. Jim took my hand and said, ' Mr. Truett, do you mean to tell me that if I surrender myself to Jesus He'll save me?' 'That's exactly what I mean.' ' But,' he said, ' I'm the worst man this side of hell, can He save me?' ' He died to save the vilest sinner this side of hell, and He'll save you if you'll surrender to Him.' ' That's right. Jim, the preacher's right,' said the men. ' If I surrender now to Him, when will He save me?' ' He will save you now, Mr. Owen, right now.' ' That's right,' said the men, ' that's right, Jim.' Then he said, ' Lord Jesus, the worst man out of hell surrenders to you just now.' Everyone was crying, the men and women kissed him, and there was great joy, for the chief of sinners had been saved, God loosed his tongue and he turned to those men and gave the most marvelous testimony I ever heard.

"For years there had been a great feud between him and another man, and the next day he went to his enemy and said, 'Friend, you're not afraid of me and I'm not afraid of you, and I've come to ask forgiveness for all the wrongs I have done you. I'm a new man now.' Thus the breach was healed, and they came together singing the praises of God."

"Friend, Jesus of Nazareth, is mighty to save."

III

THE WONDERS OF FAITH AND PRAYER

Our prayers when we pray in the Holy Ghost will be marked by strength. James tells us that "the supplication of a righteous man availeth much in its working" (James 5:16, R. V.). The word he employs in telling us this sets before us forcibly the point with which we are dealing. The prayers of him who prays in the Holy Ghost have strength (ischus,) vigour—bodily and mental. This word suggests strength in repose. Further, the prayers of him who prays in the Holy Ghost have energy (energeia). This word suggests strength in action. It is operative; it is efficient. It achieves results; it works wonders. He who prays in the Holy Ghost makes prayer, for the time being, the only business of his life. He gives himself up to it, and puts himself, mind, and heart, and will into it. So he prevails. He obtains answers. He seeks and finds, He asks and receives. He knocks and to him the door is opened.—Dr. G. H. C. MacGregor.

BISHOP HALL, in a well-known extract, thus puts the point of earnestness in its relation to the prayer of faith. "An arrow, if it be drawn up but a little way, goes not far; but if it be pulled up to the head, flies swiftly and pierces deep. Thus prayer, if it be only dribbled forth from careless lips, falls at our feet. It is the strength of strong desire which sends it to

Heaven, and makes it pierce the clouds. It is not the arithmetic of our prayers, how many they are; nor the rhetoric of our prayers, how eloquent they be; nor the geometry of our prayers, how long they be; nor the music of our prayers, how sweet our voice may be; nor the logic of our prayers, how argumentative they may be; nor even the divinity of our prayers, how good the doctrine may be, which God cares for. . . . Fervency of spirit is that which availeth much."

In an old book of sermons the preacher discusses the subject of Faith and says:

"Faith in God ennobles Reason; Unbelief degrades Reason.

"Faith in God involves in its very act a rational appreciation of evidence. (The evidence of Bible truth is so clear that man cannot reject it without folly as well as sin.)

"Faith in God promotes the highest exercise of reason because it rests upon the most substantial and durable foundation.

"Faith takes in the sublimest truths and the widest circle of thought. (Here are mines flashing with gems of richest lustre; here is a paradise where the tree of knowledge luxuriates with perennial fruits, and truths are budding now that shall effloresce in the sunny clime of heaven.)

"Guided by the philosophy of faith we shall not stumble at mysteries nor at alleged contradictions between science and revelation. (Philosophic

quaerit, theologia invenit, religio possidet verita-
tem. Said Picus of Mirandola, ' Philosophy seeks
truth, theology finds it, religion possesses it.' "

Faith is an essential condition of salvation.

Faith is essential to the enlightenment and ex-
pansion of our intellectual vision. (Faith does not
create these truths; it does not discover them; but
it accepts them as eternal verities unfolded from
the mind of God.)

Faith is essential to the refining and ennobling
of our spiritual nature.

Faith is a principle of moral discipline to edu-
cate and fit the soul for a higher state of being.

Faith is a principle pertaining to eternity as well
as time.

(To cherish infidelity is to paralyse one of the
noblest faculties of the soul.)

The simplicity, yet power, of faith is illustrated
by the following:

" I am glad there is a depth in the Bible I know
nothing about," says Mr. Moody; " that there is a
height there I cannot climb to if I should live to
be as old as Methuselah: I venture to say that if I
should live for ages on earth I would only have
touched its surface. I pity the man who knows all
the Bible, for it is a pretty good sign he doesn't
know himself. A man came to me with what he
thought was a very difficult passage, and he said:

" ' Mr. Moody, how do you explain it?'

" I said: ' I don't explain it.'

" ' But how do you interpret it? '

" ' I don't interpret it.'

" ' Well, how do you understand it? '

" ' I don't understand it.'

" ' But what do you do with it? '

" ' I don't do anything with it.'

" ' You don't believe it? '

" Yes. I believe it. There are lots of things
that I believe that I do not understand. In John
three, Christ says to Nicodemus: ' If you do not
understand earthly things, how can you understand heavenly things? ' About my own body I
do not understand. I don't understand nature;
it is filled with wonderful things I don't compre-
hend. Then why should I expect to know everything spiritually?

" But men ask, ' How can you prove the Book is
inspired? ' I answer, ' Because it inspires me.' "

That is one of the best proofs. It does inspire us.

Faith and Prayer go together.

A mighty man of prayer was David Brainerd.
In his diary we read this record: " Found some
ardour of soul in secret prayer; O that I might
grow up into the likeness of God." . . . " I was
in such anguish and pleaded with such earnestness
and importunity that when I rose from my knees I
felt extremely weak and overcome. . . . Thus I
spent the evening praying incessantly for divine
assistance." As a result of his praying he saw

mighty outpourings of the Spirit. " The power of
God seemed to descend upon the assembly like a
mighty rushing wind and with an astonishing
energy bore down all before it. I stood amazed at
the influence which seemed to seize the audience
and could compare it to nothing more aptly than
the irresistible force of a mighty torrent or swell-
ing deluge."

Fenelon, that great French saint, said: " Of all
the duties enjoined by Christianity none is more
essential and yet more neglected than prayer.
Most people consider the exercise a fatiguing cere-
mony, which they are justified in abridging as
much as possible. Even those whose professions
or fears lead them to pray, pray with such languor
and wanderings of mind that their prayers, far
from drawing down blessings, only increase their
condemnation."

John Foster, the Baptist divine, has said, " More
and better praying will bring the surest and read-
iest triumph to God's cause; feeble, formal, listless
praying brings decay and death. The Church has
its sheet anchor in the closet; its magazine stores
are there . . . when the Church of God is aroused
to its obligation and duties, and right faith to claim
what Christ has promised—all things whatsoever
—a revolution will take place."

It was said of Luther's prayer life that " Not a
day passes in which he does not employ in prayer
at least three of his very best hours." Someone

listening to him in prayer said, "Whilst I was listening to Luther praying in this manner at a distance, my soul seemed on fire within me to hear the man address God so like a friend yet with such gravity and reverence; and also to hear him in the course of his prayer, insisting on the promises contained in the Psalms as if he were sure his petitions would be granted."

"I tell the Lord my troubles and difficulties and wait for Him to give me the answers to them," says one man of God. "And it is wonderful how a matter that looked very dark will in prayer become clear as crystal by the help of God's Spirit. I think Christians fail so often to get answers to their prayers because they do not wait long enough on God. They just drop down and pray a few words and then jump up and forget it, and expect God to answer them. Such praying always reminds me of the small boy ringing his neighbour's door-bell and then running away as fast as he can go."

The prayer of faith is the only power in the universe to which the great Jehovah yields. Prayer is the sovereign remedy.

There are three degrees in prayer—saying prayers, praying and prevailing in prayer. To prevail in prayer, we must understand that prayer is conflict. "Orare est laborare," cried Luther. It is said of Jesus, "and being in an agony, he prayed more earnestly." Isaiah 64:7 mourns that there

is no one stirring up himself to take hold of God.
Truly has one said, " Prayer is the putting forth
of the utmost energy of character in earnest desire,
making fullest and strongest demand upon God.
Prayer needs the whole energy of man, but at the
same moment his whole nature must be sustained,
pervaded, animated by the divine spirit, who himself fills man with his own energy." St. Catherine
told a friend that the anguish she experienced in
the realisation of the sufferings of Christ was
greatest at the moment she was pleading for the
salvation of others. Thus, to her, prevailing
prayer meant anguish of soul.

Prayer is both subjective and objective. Henry
Ward Beecher exemplified wonderfully in his pulpit prayers, the subjective element in prayer. It is
said that the effect of his prayers was magical upon
the great throng. It would seem while Mr.
Beecher was praying that each one in the church
was taken in his arms and borne into the presence
of that God who was waiting to be gracious.
Many said that after the prayer they did not seem
to need the sermon. Their weary, yearning, dis-
satisfied spirits had obtained rest, satisfaction and
peace. But prayer is objective, and this we would
say with emphasis. Prayer not only calms and
soothes and comforts, but it brings wonderful
things to pass. Heine, the German philosopher
and skeptic, once said: " When men call for
help on the unseen, no one but a fool expects

an answer." This is the rationalistic view of prayer, but we believe that it is the highest wisdom to pray fervently and believingly, and expect to get things from God in answer to prayer. God's people have prayed for money, and money has come. They have prayed for help, and help has been given. They have prayed for friends, and friends have arrived. They have prayed for open doors, and doors have been opened. They have prayed for health and it was given. They have prayed for food and clothing, and it came. In a thousand or more ways God, the mighty God, has listened to the cries of His children and answered in ways miraculous, mysterious and marvelous.

Here is a remarkable answer to prayer. Dr. Talmage says:

" In the winter of 1875 we were worshipping in the Brooklyn Academy of Music. We had great audiences, but I was oppressed beyond measure by the fact that conversions were not numerous. On Tuesday I invited to my house five old consecrated Christian men. These old men came not knowing why I had invited them. I took them to the top room of my house. I said to them, ' I have called you here for special prayer. I am in agony for a great turning to God of the people. We have vast multitudes in attendance, and they are attentive and respectful, but I cannot see that they are saved. Let us kneel down and each one pray, and not leave this room until we are all assured that the blessing will come, and has come.' It was a most intense crying unto God. I said, ' Brethren, let this meeting be a secret,' and they said, ' It will be.' That next Friday night came the usual prayer-meeting. No one knew what had occurred on Tuesday night, but the meeting was unusually thronged. Men accustomed to pray in public with great composure broke down under emotion. The people were in tears. There were sobs and silences and solemnities of such unusual power that the worshippers looked into each others' faces as much as to say, ' What does all this mean?' And when the following Sabbath came, although we were in a secular place, over 400 arose for prayers, and a religious awakening took place that made that winter memorable."

A most extraordinary answer to prayer.

Miss Jennie Hughes and Dr. Mary Stone, of China, who, because of their refusal to submit to the demands of Modernism resigned from the . . . . Missionary Society of the . . . . Church, after seventeen years' faithful labours, are now doing a remarkable work in Shanghai, China, along independent lines. In a recent letter Miss Hughes tells a most remarkable story. It reads like a romance, but it shows how wonderfully God will provide a way when every door is shut. The *Eastern Methodist* published the incident thus:

" The following interesting incident is taken from a recent letter from Miss Jennie Hughes: ' This place is situated at Arsenal Road, so called because the Arsenal and a huge barrack are there. When we first came we were told it would not be safe—that this was the wildest part of Shanghai— that the soldiers would molest the nurses, etc. But we felt we had been guided in coming, so left all such questions to God. We had not been here long when we so much wished we could begin evangelistic work among the soldiers, but as we were all women and did not have even a native pastor of our own, we could not gain entrance to the barracks.

" ' Well, one day I was having a room cleaned out where some of the boarding school pupils slept, and among their last year's dilapidated school books I found a torn Bible, just a part of the New Testament. I gave all the scraps of various kinds to the coolie to burn, but as he was preparing to light the fire, one of the prowling, semi-wild dogs that abound all over China ran in and, grabbing the Bible in his mouth, made off with it. We did not know the sequel till quite a while afterward. Then we learned that the dog ran down the road and dashed between the sentries at the gate into the courtyard of the barracks. Some soldiers who had nothing to do chased him to find out what he had in his mouth, and when they got the torn book they sat down and read it. None of them had ever seen a Bible, though they had heard of it, and they all read all there was in it. The next Sunday, when Dr. Stone was leading the morning service, she was amazed to see two officers and a group of soldiers come into the church and sit down at the back. They were the ones who had read the dog's Bible, and they have been coming ever since. Their wives and children are now Dr. Mary's patients, and an entrance has been effected into the military community. Is not that just as wonderful as Elijah and the ravens?' "

IV

SIN AND SALVATION

The old Theology of sin seems to be dying and in its place the rudest creeds, spiritualism, theosophy, mystic mummery, New Theology and infidelity spring up carrying multitudes to ruin and hell. Too often is sin set in fair forms and dazzling colours. The seduction of many a soul is wrought by poetry and its ruin by music. We may be poisoned with roses and our corruption be covered by a cloth of gold, and the pathway of ruin may be strewn with flowers. Our very shames may glow with delusive lustre and dazzle the sight. A brilliant spider on the Amazon spreads itself out like a flower and attracts to their torment and death multitudes of insects. Souls are deceived and ruined by the legerdemain of passion and fancy. "The power of imagination may purge the darkest sins into lily whiteness, perfume it with violet and steep it in the colour of the rose."—W. L. WATKINSON.

IT is said of Thomas Boston, that great preacher of the long ago, that often his language was tasked and strained to the utmost when he would preach on "Redemptive Blessings," which as he understood them and proclaimed them with a full soul, met "all men's necessities; the full and irrevocable forgiveness of sins; reinstatement in the divine favour and friendship; the gift of the Holy Spirit in his enlighten-

45

ing, purifying and peace-giving influences, turning
men into living temples of the Living God."

It was a saying of Jerome that "he that hath
slight thoughts of sin never had great thoughts of
God." We must confess with Jowett that "we do
not like some of the stern, bare, jagged words
which our fathers used in their description of sin."
There is a kind of psychology around today that is
inflicting death wounds to our theology and a lot
of thinking and teaching that would interpret
human need "as though it were a skin complaint
and not a heart disease." As a result of this ex-
punged and devitalised theology "the consciences
of the people are being stroked with feathers
dipped in oil."

It is a noteworthy fact that the preachers every-
where in every age and time who have been the
most evangelical, the most successful in winning
souls and whose ministry has blessed their age and
generation have all been men who have held a
vigourous Pauline and Johannine doctrine of sin.
From Augustine down to Billy Sunday this is so.
The man whose doctrine of sin is defective will be
defective all along the line of his theology, and
undoubtedly one of the troubles of our age is a
sadly defective theology of sin. Damage the
doctrine of sin and you damage the doctrine of
the atonement; damage that and your Christology
becomes impaired; damage that and the inspiration
and authority of your Bible suffers also, and thus

it goes on till all goes and faith suffers complete
wreckage.

True words were those of Jowett: " You cannot expunge the theology and retain the morality;
a devitalised theology creates a disabled and dis-
pirited morality; impoverish your creed and you
sterilise your morality."

There are on the whole three schools of thought
upon the sin question.

1. Those who teach that sin lies in the wrong
action of the will and that there is no moral depravity from which we need salvation.   This is
Pelagianism.

2. Those who hold that sin is constitutional and
involves voluntary transgression and guilt, but we
cannot be made entirely free from sin in this life.
This is Calvinism.

3. Those who hold that man is born with a
corrupt   nature   (depravity)   and   becomes   an
actual transgressor involving condemnation and
guilt, but through divine grace can be fully saved
from sin in this life.   This is Arminianism or
Methodism.

The first and second views of sin tend to make
allowance for sin and furnish many opportunities
to speak of the " corruptions in their heart, in an
unaffected and airy manner, as if they talked of
freckles upon their faces and to run down their
sinful nature only to apologise for their sinful
practices; or to appear great proficients in self-

knowledge and count the praise due to genuine humility."

The Methodist doctrine of sin tells the secret of our success in getting multitudes saved. We have preached that human nature is corrupt and men have sinned grievously against God, bringing on them guilt and condemnation. This has produced conviction and penitence and repentance, the only conditions of soul which God can bless with a salvation that abundantly pardons the transgressor and cleanses from all sin. The history of Methodism is written in tears of the penitent, sobs of the contrite, joys of the converted and shouts of the sanctified, and hallelujahs of the redeemed!

Fundamental in our doctrine of sin is conviction for sin. A recent tract of Modernism on "How May I Become a Christian?" (published by the Department of Evangelism) has the following:

"To become a Christian one actually sets out to accomplish aggressively certain goals." . . . "The man who would become a Christian must be willing to believe *good things about God and about himself*." . . . "When one makes an honest effort to think good things about God and himself he will naturally turn to Jesus Christ, who is the 'outstanding expert.'" . . . "The moment a man musters the might of his will and acts—crusades—discovers God by means of the life of Jesus and becomes a friend of Christ at that moment he becomes a Christian though it takes a lifetime to complete the task."

This tract throws into discard everything evangelical and Biblical. It is Unitarian. It ignores the fact of guilt *and has no place for conviction of sin*. It looks upon Christ as an " outstanding expert," but fails to honour Him as " Mighty to Save," a wonderful Saviour, and totally ignores the blood of Jesus, but what we must consider as fundamental in the Gospel is the fact of sin and *Conviction for Sin*. Dr. Buckley said:

" It is the fashion among some Christians to think that painful experiences of conviction are felt only by weak, ignorant, and superstitious persons. But this is not the case. Augustine was not weak or ignorant. He was a scholar and a philosopher, a man of powerful intellect. Jonathan Edwards was neither a weak nor ignorant man. William Wilberforce was not a weak man. John Bunyan was not educated in the ordinary sense of that term, but he was a man of remarkable talents and extraordinary good sense. All these men experienced the deepest anguish of soul on account of sin. They felt as though their sins had plunged them into a bottomless abyss of misery. Daniel Webster was not a weak man. Americans delight to honour him as a man of rare intellectual powers and statesmanlike grasp of thought. It is well known that he was not a real Christian in his life. When asked what was the greatest thought he ever had, he replied, 'In my opinion the greatest thought that ever entered a human mind is man's personal accountability to God.' It is said that Mr. Webster, on his dying bed, repeated the whole of that penitential hymn of Isaac Watts which is sung in nearly all the churches:

> " ' Show pity, Lord; O Lord, forgive!
> Let a repenting rebel live;
> Are not Thy mercies large and free?
> May not a sinner trust in Thee?
>
> " ' My crimes are great, but don't surpass
> The power and glory of Thy grace;
> Great God, Thy nature hath no bound,
> So let Thy pardoning love be found.
>
> " ' O wash my soul from every sin,
> And make my guilty conscience clean;
> Here on my heart the burden lies,
> And past offenses pain mine eyes.
>
> " ' My lips with shame my sins confess
> Against Thy law, against Thy grace;
> Lord, should Thy judgments grow severe,
> I am condemned, but Thou art clear.' "

When George Mueller was under conviction he said:

" Never in my whole life had I seen myself so vile, so guilty, so altogether what I ought not to have been, as at this time. It was as if every sin of which I had been guilty was brought to my remembrance; but at the same time I could realise that all my sins were completely forgiven—that I was washed and made clean, completely clean, in the blood of Jesus. The result of this was great peace."

John Wesley furnishes us a striking example of conviction for sin. We see this man—M. A. of Oxford, Clergyman of the Established Church, Missionary to Georgia returning to London, mourning over his lost condition thus:

" This then have I learned in the ends of the earth: That I am fallen short of the glory of God; that my whole heart is altogether corrupt and abominable, and consequently my whole life (seeing it cannot be, that an evil tree should bring forth good fruit), that alienated as I am from the life of God, I am a child of wrath, an heir of hell; that my own works, my own sufferings, my own righteousness, are so far from reconciling me to an offended God, so far from making any atonement for the least of those sins, which are more in number than the hairs of my head, that the most specious of them need an atonement themselves, or they cannot abide His righteous judgment; that having the sentence of death in my heart, and having nothing in or of myself to plead, I have no hope, but that of being justified freely ' through the redemption that is in Jesus.' I have no hope but that if I seek I shall find Christ, and ' be found in him, not having my own righteousness, but that which is through the faith of Christ: the righteousness which is of God by faith.'

" I see that the whole law of God is holy, just
and good. I know every thought, every temper of
my soul, ought to bear God's image and super-
scription. But how am I fallen from the glory of
God! I feel that 'I am sold under sin.' I know
that I, too, deserve nothing but wrath, being full
of all abominations; and having no good thing in
me, to atone for them or to remove the wrath of
God. All my works, my righteousness, my prayers, need an atonement for themselves. So that
my mouth is stopped. I have nothing to plead.
God is holy; I am unholy. God is a consum-
ing fire; I am altogether a sinner, meet to be
consumed."

The state of the unsaved soul is further illustrated by the following incident:

A brilliant young physician came up to an evangelist after a meeting in Kansas, a few years ago,
and said: " I am tied to my mother's apron strings.
I have always lived up to her teachings, morally,
and I pride myself on the fact that while I was
away in the medical institution, where I received
high honours, I kept myself clean. I do not pro-
fess to be a Christian, but I am a better moral man
than any of the Church members of this city."
" Doctor," the evangelist replied, " I do not doubt
you for an instant, but I want your attention.
Unregeneracy is a state. You have not been regenerated, have you? " He replied, " No, sir, I do
not claim to be a regenerated man." They were

standing together in the aisle, and the evangelist, drawing a square in the sawdust, said: " Doctor, let this square represent the State of Colorado." He said, " All right." He continued, " The altitude at the lowest point is 2,000 feet above the sea level; the highest altitude, the summit of Pike's Peak, is 14,200 feet above the sea level; and there are people in the Colorado mines who are 3,000 feet below the lowest altitude in the State. Whether they are in the mines, on the lowest altitude, or on the summit of Pike's Peak, they are all in the State of Colorado. Now the state of unregeneracy is like that. Some men are away down below the surface in the underground villainy and criminality of flagrant wickedness; others range about the ordinary surfacing, the lowest altitude in the state of unregeneracy; while you are on the summit of Mount Morality; *but you are all in the state of unregeneracy."* The young physician looked at the evangelist for a moment in dumb amazement, and then said, without a word of argument—" You have knocked the props out from under me; I am with you! " and he walked down the aisle to the place of prayer, where he publicly confessed Jesus Christ as his personal Saviour.

Turning now to Salvation, what are its characteristics?

It is a salvation that has God for its author, and originated before the foundation of the world. Eph. 1: 4.

It is a salvation that found is necessity in man's sin and his lost condition. Rom. 3:23.

It is a salvation that provides freedom from sin and demands holiness. Rom. 6:22.

It is a salvation that is of faith and not of works. Eph. 2:8-9.

It is an uttermost salvation. Heb. 7:25.

It is a present salvation and eternal.

This salvation effects the sinner's conversion. Professor James, in speaking of conversion, says: "To be converted, to be regenerated, to receive grace, to experience religion, to gain assurance, are so many phrases which denote the process, gradual or sudden, by which a self hitherto divided, and consciously wrong, inferior and unhappy, becomes unified and consciously right, superior and happy, in consequence of its firmer hold upon religious realities." Quoting another eminent writer, Professor James records his words as follows: "I am bold to say that the work of God in the conversion of one soul, considered together with the source, foundation, and purchase of it, and also the benefit and eternal issue of it, is a more glorious work of God than the creation of the whole material universe."

Conversion from a Scriptural standpoint means being "born again," John 3:3, being made a "new creature," 2 Cor. 5:17, Gal. 6:15; passing "from death unto life," John 5:24, 1 John 3:14;

translation from the power of darkness into the
Kingdom of His dear Son, Col. 1:13. Wesley
defines it as "that great change which God works
in the soul when He brings it into life; when He
raises it from the death of sin to the life of righteousness. It is the change wrought in the whole
soul by the Almighty Spirit of God when it is
created anew in Christ Jesus; when it is renewed
after the image of God in righteousness and true
holiness."

This is further enforced by John Wesley's own
experience. When converted, on the night of May
24, 1738, he says: "I felt my heart strangely
warmed. I felt I did trust in Christ, alone, for my
salvation; and an assurance was given me, that he
had taken away my sins, even mine, and saved me
from the law of sin and death; and I then testified
openly to all there what I now first felt in my
heart."

Eighteen days afterwards he preached at St.
Mary's, Oxford, a sermon from the text, "By
grace are ye saved, through faith," in the course
of which he said: "Faith is a full reliance on the
blood of Christ, and a trust in the merits of His
life, death, and resurrection—a *recumbency* upon
Him as our atonement and our life, as given for
us and living in us; and, in consequence hereof, a
closing with Him and cleaving to Him as our
wisdom, righteousness, sanctification, redemption,
or in one word, our salvation."

Furthermore this Salvation secures to the believers the experience of Full Salvation.

Flavel has said: " What the heart is to the body, that the soul is to the man, and what health is to the heart, holiness is to the soul."

Holiness is health. Holiness is wholeness. Holiness is cleansing. Holiness is soundness. Holiness is happiness. We are chosen for Holiness. Eph. 1:4. We are called to Holiness, 2 Tim. 1:9. We are commanded to be holy, 1 Pet. 2:16. Again, to quote John Wesley, we hear him say:

" When I began to make the Scriptures my study (about seven and twenty years ago), I began to see that Christians are called to love God with all their heart and to serve Him with all their strength, which is precisely what I apprehend is meant by the scriptural term perfection. After weighing this for some years, I openly declared my sentiments on the Circumcision of the Heart. About six years after, an advice I received from Bishop Gibson, ' Tell all the world what you mean by perfection,' I publish my coolest and latest thoughts in the sermon on that subject. I therein build on no authority, ancient or modern, but the Scripture."

" But none can attain perfection unless they first believe it is attainable. neither do I affirm this. I knew a Calvinist in London who never believed it attainable till the moment she did attain it; and then lay declaring it aloud for many days, till her spirit returned to God."

"As to the word perfection, it is Scriptural; therefore, neither you nor I can in conscience object to it, unless we would send the Holy Ghost to school, and teach him to speak who made the tongue."

"What then does their arguing reprove, who object against Christian Perfection? Absolute or infallible perfection I never contended for. Sinless perfection I do not contend for, seeing that it is not Scriptural. A perfection, such as enables a person to fulfill the whole law, and so needs not the merits of Christ. I acknowledge no such perfection; I do now, and always did, protest against it."

V

GOD'S SKIES ARE FULL OF
PENTECOSTS

I stood a little while ago on the banks and watched the great Falls of Niagara as they roared and tumbled and pushed on with a momentum marvelous, and thought of the power at work there. One man looking on the sight one day exclaimed: " There is the greatest unused power in the world." A Christian man replied, " No, the greatest unused power on earth is the power of the Holy Ghost." One has said, " The gift of the Holy Ghost is a vital, spiritual power which, in its burning energy, purifies and transforms those whom it possesses, and fills them also with a divine anointing effectual in its manifestations to the regeneration and transforming of many."

THE Day of Pentecost is a day full of the most vital significance because it commemorates the great gift when the Holy Spirit was outpoured on the Apostles and members of the Church at Jerusalem. Augustine called this day the " dies natalis " of the Holy Ghost and said: " It is evident that the present dispensation under which we are, is the dispensation of the Spirit of the Third Person of the Holy Trinity. To Him in the divine economy has been committed the office of applying the Redemption of the Son to the souls of men by the vocation, justification, and salvation of the elect. We are therefore under the personal guidance of the Third Person as the Apostles were under the guidance of the Second."

Pentecost was God's greatest gift to His Church next to that of His Son and His atoning work through His precious blood shed upon Calvary. It was an event effusive and diffusive. The lambent flame gave new lustre to things divine and lit the torch of gospel truth to lighten ages and epochs and peoples and nations. The Spirit was given in power and fire and inflamed and energised all upon whom He fell. There swept out into Jerusalem, into Samaria, into the regions round about, into Greece and Rome, flames of holy fire that kindled revivals whose history is read in the Acts and Epistles, and which have been repeated since in Luther's day and Wesley's and Moody's and Inskip's and our own.

Pentecost was a promise fulfilled, a prayer answered, a vision realised, a power bestowed, a fire kindled, an energy set free, a current set in motion, a river set flowing, a Spirit sent forth, a new song and joy to the Church, and a power victorious.

It broke upon the Church, on Sunday morning, and ever since Sunday has been a Day Divine. It broke upon the preacher, and ever since the preacher has been the man with messages that burn. It broke upon praying believers, and ever since prayer has been a means wonderful. It broke upon the Church, and ever since the Church has been the House of Blessing, and the scene of the Spirit's effusion. Applied to the truth, pentecostal power has made it a hammer to break hard hearts, a sword to pierce the conscience, a fire to burn out sin. Applied to the Church, pentecostal power has made it a place of healing to diseased souls, of salvation to the sinner, of peace to the disconsolate, of revelation to searchers after truth, and a place of vision.

Pentecost was Christ's greatest gift to the Church. Its fiery tongues lit up the promises of God, burned away barriers, and purged clean the hearts of the disciples. It made Peter a preacher on fire, who won three thousand souls in one sermon. Pentecostal fire burned in Philip's heart, and he evangelised Samaria. It burned in Stephen, and with firelit face he prayed for those who stoned him. It turned a Saul of Tarsus into Paul, the great apostle, and pentecostal fire swept in to Athens and Corinth, and Ephesus, and burned its way to the Roman throne, and thus touched all the world.

Pentecostal fire touched Luther, and Protestantism sprang forth. It touched the Wesleys and Whitefield, and they sang and preached and prayed in the great Revival of the Centuries. It burned in Edward's soul, and behold, the Great Awakening. In Moody, and Sankey, and lo, a new evangelism. In Inskip, and Cookman, in Evan

Roberts, and lo, the Welsh revival, in Chapman and Gypsy Smith, and a new righteousness sprang forth.

"God's skies are full of pentecosts," exclaimed Bishop Warren. Let the Church of today seek it, and power will flow, that will turn weakness into strength, darkness into light, sorrow into joy, and defeat into victory.

Rev. Thomas Waugh, the great preacher, Evangelist of English Methodism, tells how he came to realise his Pentecost, in his autobiography, thus: "I saw very clearly that after Pentecost those early Christians had a fullness of Divine life and Power to which I was a stranger. I realised that while I had the Spirit, I was not filled with the Spirit; that I had welcomed Him as guest, but not yet as host, in my heart. I also saw that this glorious fullness was as much for poor me as for Peter, James and John. In New Testament plentitude, however, the Holy Spirit could not come until Christ had ascended. Until He was glorified, the Church could not have her Pentecost; and what is true of the Church is true of the individual Christian. I saw that some of my ambitions would have to perish, but I could hold out no longer. My whole being looked up to God and said: 'None of self and all for Thee; I want what those early Christians got at Pentecost. It is my birthright in Jesus, and for me as for them; I need it as much as they did; I am willing, and claim and trust.' I shall never forget that hour. There was no joyous exultation or deep inrush of emotion, but a great calm. I kept on trusting; then the signs and wonders of my longings, hopes and prayers began to come. Within twenty months I saw 1,800 souls led to Christ, and since then those numbers have reached nearly 90,000 men, women, and children."

The paramount lesson of Pentecost is obtained as we study it in the light of the Holy Spirit and His work. We might well ask as we contemplate those things: Has the Holy Spirit that place in the affairs of the Church and ministry that He should have? Are we experiencing His power as did our fathers? Dr. Daniel Steele, that man of keen spiritual vision and of divinely deep experience in the " deep things of God," wrote one day these words: " The trend of modern Protestantism is towards a growing feebleness of grasp upon the Holy Spirit as a reality, and a practical disuse of this source of spiritual life and power."

The Spirit of God is the *Spirit of Conviction.* Stephen Grellet, that extraordinary man of the Quaker Church, was brought up a Roman Catholic. Whilst walking along the Hudson one day not thinking of serious matters he was suddenly arrested by the word: " Eternity, Eternity, Eternity," sounding through his soul. At once eternal things became real to him,—he went to prayer and ceased not till he found pardon at the cross. It was the Spirit of the Lord.

The Spirit of God convicts of sin, of righteousness, and of judgment to come. He shows that self-righteousness is as filthy rags, that sinners must be stripped of every false hope, they must have their refuge of lies destroyed, they must see themselves as bankrupt and lost before God, that there is no hope outside the Cross. This leads to a true repentance which involves hatred of sin, confession of sin and the sincere abandonment of all known wrong.

Touching the Spirit's work in regeneration and saving faith Bishop Moule says: " The Holy Spirit is the Spirit of Faith. He leads to saving faith. The convicted soul must *will* to believe, he must *choose* to believe, he must *determine* to believe, that ' Jesus saves me now.' " Dougan Clarke, that lucid Quaker writer, has said: " Faith is the acceptance of God's mercy and grace in Christ Jesus. The grace of faith or the power of believing is the gift of God. . . . To every contrite anxious soul that *wills to believe* the power to do so will be given by the Holy Ghost."

The Holy Spirit is the Witnessing Spirit. This was one of the peculiar doctrines of Methodism,— the witness of the Spirit. John Wesley defines the witness in the following language: " By the testimony of the Spirit I mean an inward impression on the soul, whereby the Spirit of God immediately and directly witnesses to my spirit that I am a child of God, that Jesus Christ hath loved me and given Himself for me, that all my sins are blotted out, and I, even I, am reconciled to God. I do not mean hereby that the Spirit of God testifies this by an outward voice. No, nor always by an inward voice, although He may do this sometimes. Neither do I suppose that He always applies to the heart (although He often may) one or more texts of Scripture. But He so works upon the soul by His immediate influence and by a strong though inexplicable operation, that the stormy wind and the troubled waves subside, and there is a sweet calm, the heart resting in Jesus, and the sinner being clearly satisfied that all his iniquities are forgiven and his sins covered."

The Holy Spirit is the Praying Spirit. Romans 8:26. "Likewise the Spirit also helpeth our infirmities, for we know not what we should pray for as we ought, but the Spirit itself maketh intercession for us with groanings which cannot be uttered." "The blessed Spirit frameth our intercession for us within, His prayer is an inner prayer within our prayer, a silent Divine voice within our voice, the soul of which our prayer is the body" (Whedon). The Holy Spirit suggests and prompts prayer in the believer's heart and accompanies it with a corresponding faith. A Christian lady was strongly moved to pray for a suffering friend. She went to her room and poured out her heart in fervent supplication. Whilst in prayer the thought came to her, "Cannot I send her a telegram by way of Heaven?" "and in full faith" she said, "I asked the Lord to bring this passage to her mind: 'As one whom his mother comforteth so will I comfort you.'" In a few days word was received that just at that same hour the "telegram" by way of Heaven reached the friend in distress and she was sweetly calmed and her mourning brought to an end.

"If we remain constantly surrendered to God, and looking to Jesus," says a Quaker writer, "He will show us by the Holy Spirit when and how to pray the true prayer of faith, and this is praying in the Holy Ghost."

The Holy Spirit is the Baptismal Spirit. "Ye shall be baptised with the Holy Ghost," said Jesus. Dr. Asa Mahan, in his great work on the Holy Spirit, teaches us that "the Holy Spirit having first builded us for a habitation of God, at our conversion, then proceeds with a process of preparation and sanctification which is more or less gradual, but need not be long, and when this is completed if we are consecrated and inquiring of Him to do it for us, God takes possession of the temple, in His glory and His power, by the baptism with the Holy Ghost."

A great soul winner was that eminent Christian, Professor Tholuck, of Halle, Germany, many years ago. When he went to that institution infidelity was rampant. His Christian influence was wonderful upon the students. He won hundreds of them to Christ.   He gave the secret of his power in these words: "I have but one passion, and that is Christ and Christ alone.   All my success has been owing to the baptism of fire which I received at the very commencement of my public career and to the principle of love that seeks and follows."

Shortly after Charles G. Finney's conversion he received a wonderful baptism of the Holy Spirit. This it was which endued him and qualified him for that marvelous evangelistic career during which he stirred the whole country for God.   Oh for a like baptism!   "We have our instruments for pulling down the stronghold, but Oh, for the baptism of fire!" cried Rev. W. Arthur, author of "The Tongue of Fire."   Dr. Torrey says: "Religious biographies abound in instances of men who have worked along as best they could, until one day they were led to see that there was such an experience as the baptism with the Holy Spirit and to seek it and obtain it, and from that hour, there came into their service a new power that utterly transformed its character."   Such an experience was that of Dr. A. T. Pierson when pastor of a large Presbyterian Church in Detroit.   He saw and sought his privilege in the Spirit's Baptism.   He testified thus: "For sixteen years I preached the gospel with all the logic and rhetoric I could command.   The results were disappointing.   An untutored evangelist came to our city.   Hundreds were swept into the kingdom by his simple story of the gospel. Then my eyes were opened. I saw that the secret of his power lay in his possession of the Holy Spirit. After praying that I might receive His power, it came on me November 15th. In the following sixteen months I made more converts than I had gained in the previous sixteen years."

A very eminent Methodist preacher, scholar, and saint, said; " I made the discovery that I was living in the pre-pentecostal state of religious experience, admiring Christ's character, obeying His law, and in a degree loving His person, but without the conscious blessing of the Comforter. I settled the question of privilege by a study of John's Gospel and St. Paul's Epistles and earnestly sought for the Comforter. I prayed, consecrated, confessed my state, and believed Christ's word. Very suddenly, after three weeks' diligent search, the Comforter came with power and great joy to my heart. He took my feet out of the road of doubt and weakness and planted them forever on the rock of assurance and strength."

VI

DOUBLE PORTION OF THE SPIRIT

"Christianity," says one, "is nothing if it be not supernatural." Prayer is a supernatural power. It is one of the great potential forces of the kingdom. We might well marvel at the mystery and the greatness of its power, but "Mont Blanc does not become a phantom or a mist because a climber grows dizzy on its side."

Professor William James, of Harvard, who was more eminent as a Psychologist than as a Christian believer, has the following to say about prayer: "The fundamental religious point is that in prayer spiritual energy which otherwise would slumber does become active and spiritual work of some kind is effected really."

THE measure of people's spirituality may be determined by the spirit of their praying and the nature and object of their desire. A story is told of John Fletcher that having done some worthy deed to one of England's aristocracy the recipient addressed a letter of gratitude to Fletcher and at the same time requested him to name what he wanted in return. Fletcher's reply was to the effect that there was but one thing he needed most and that was *"more grace."* When we recollect what a man of God Fletcher was we come to understand why he preferred more grace to all that earth could bestow. In this Scripture we are assured that Elisha was a man of God. He shows it by his prayer. As his master Elijah is about to leave him he asks not for wealth—Elijah had none to give him. Nor does he request earthly honours,—these Elijah had none to bestow; but Elisha desires but one thing—*A spiritual endowment.*

Let us learn a few lessons concerning the Spirit's enduement.

1. That a double portion of the Spirit is the special privilege of all God's children. Deut. 21:17 tells us that the first-born son had a right to a double portion. There is a sense in which all who are born of God have the same prerogative. Certain it is that every Christian has the Spirit's portion in pardon and adoption. He may have the Spirit's double portion in entire cleansing and baptism of power.

2. The double portion of the Spirit is required to meet the *double effect* of sin and transgression. Isaiah 1:18 intimates that sinners are double dyed —a figure borrowed possibly from the ancient custom of dyeing an article *twice*, dyeing it first, then drying it, then dyeing it the second time. So is the case of every man. He is double-dyed in sin, born in sin, and with sin, and then a sinner by actual transgression and practices. The double portion— the double work is therefore needed to meet the sad necessities of the case. In justification the soul is pardoned and cleansed of its actual transgres-

sions; in sanctification it is cleansed from its indwelling sin. By the grace and experience of holiness we mean "That renewal of our fallen nature by the Holy Ghost whereby we are washed entirely from sin's pollution, freed from its power and are enabled through grace to love God with all our hearts and to walk in His holy Commandments blameless."

3. The Spirit's double portion is the best qualification for Christian work and service.

The effect of the Spirit's outpouring upon Christian workers has the following characteristics:

(a) Promotes Prayerfulness.

Charles Wesley puts the plea for the praying spirit in beautiful form when he sang,

> "Come in thy pleading Spirit down
>   To us who for thy coming stay;
> Of all thy gifts we ask but one,
>   We ask the constant power to pray;
> Indulge us, Lord, in this request,
>   Thou canst not then deny the rest."

"The constant power to pray" certainly may be put in the category of the "best gifts" which Paul urges us to covet.

> "Satan trembles when he sees
> The weakest saint upon his knees."

And well he might because the prayerful soul brings Heaven and earth together, pulls down power from the skies, obtains promises, brings things to pass.

Commissioner McKie, of the Salvation Army, used to spend his Saturday nights in prayer and his success as a soul saver was marvelous. Bramwell, the great saint, spent six hours a day.

"Christianity," says one, "is nothing if it be not supernatural." Prayer is a supernatural power. It is one of the great potential forces of the Kingdom. We might well marvel at the mystery and the greatness of its power, but "Mont Blanc does not become a phantom or a mist because a climber grows dizzy on its side."

Professor William James, of Harvard, who was more eminent as a Psychologist than as a Christian believer, has the following to say about prayer: "The fundamental religious point is that in prayer spiritual energy which otherwise would slumber does become active and spiritual work of some kind is effected really." Truly "spiritual work of some kind is effected really in prayer."

Let Jacob speak and he will tell of victory at the brook Jabbok; let Moses speak and he will tell of mighty manifestations of God; let Hannah speak and she will tell of joy born at the altar of prayer; let Elijah testify and he will tell of fire and flood; let Daniel speak and he will tell that unceasing prayer brought deliverance even in the lion's den; let Peter and Paul testify and they will tell how prayer opened prison doors and brought visions of God; let Luther speak and he will tell of prayer that brought on a reformation; let George Mueller speak and he will tell of houses and lands, and food and clothing, for thousands of orphans, all in answer to prayer; let J. Hudson Taylor, of China, Wm. Carey, of India, and Bishop Wm. Taylor, the World Missionary, speak, and they will tell of countries and continents victoriously contested for the Kingdom of God. " Prayer makes the darkened clouds withdraw. Prayer climbs the ladder Jacob saw; gives exercise to faith and love, brings every blessing from above. Prayer keeps the Christian's armour bright, and Satan trembles when he sees the weakest saint upon his knees."

4. The Double Portion begets Courage and Holy Passion.

The Spirit's enduement makes the weak strong, the timid courageous. It changed a vacillating, cringing Simon into a Peter the apostle and the mighty spokesman of the Pentecost. It delivers from fear of faces, consequences, appearances. Its only consideration is, What does God think and say? What does He require me to do? The baptism of the Spirit is a baptism of non-conformity to this old wicked world and its customs. It is that which if a man has he ceases " pouring the waters of concession into the bottomless buckets of expediency."

Emerson craved what we believe the Spirit's baptism bestows, when he wrote: " We must be baptised again into the Spirit of non-conformity, of intellectual and moral honesty, the Spirit which does not suffer men to go with the crowd when reason and conscience and a living God bid them go alone." We may well pray against "those dead calms, that flat and hopeless lull, in which the dull sea rots around the helpless bark."

One has said, " No heart is pure that is not passionate, no virtue is safe that is not enthusiastic." And another has written " Nothing great is possible in this world without that white heat of enthusiasm which makes the world consider the saints mad." And yet another has uttered a great truth in saying, " God's magnet is a man electrified by the Spirit of God." Such were the apostles, the men who "turned the world upside down," and Luther, who said of himself, ' I am rough, boisterous, stormy and altogether warlike "; and the Wesleys whom the Bishop of London called " young raw heads." William Lloyd Garretson said, " The world is full of careful people who are sinking into unremembered graves, while here and there a man forgets himself into immortality."

5. The Double Portion Produces Unworldliness.

" Be ye holy in all manner of conversation." It was the prayer of McCheyne, of Dundee, " O God, make me as holy as a pardoned sinner can be made." The Christian is not of this world, nor of the things in it. The difference between a worldly professor of religion and a real professor may be judged from the following incident told by Mr. Finney :

"In my early Christian life I heard a Methodist bishop from the South report a case that made a deep impression on my mind. He said there was in his neighbourhood a slaveholder, a gentleman of fortune, who was a gay and agreeable man, and gave himself to various field sports and amusements. He used to associate much with his pastor, often invite him to dinner, and to accompany him in his sports and pleasure-seeking excursions of various kinds. The minister cheerfully complied with these requests; and a friendship grew up between the parishioner that continued till the last sickness of this gay and wealthy man.

"When the wife of this worldling was apprised that her husband could live but a short time she was much alarmed for his soul, and tenderly inquired if she should not call in their minister to converse and pray with him. He feelingly replied, 'No, my dear; he is not the man for me to see now. He was my companion, as you know, in worldly sports and pleasure-seeking; he loves good dinners and a jolly time. I then enjoyed his society and found him a pleasant companion. But I see now that I never had any real confidence in his piety, and have now no confidence in the efficacy of his prayers. I am a dying man, and need the instruction and prayers of somebody that can prevail with God. We have been much together, but our pastor has never been serious with me about the salvation of my soul and he is not the man to help me now.'

"The wife was greatly affected, and said: 'What shall I do then?' He replied, 'My coachman, Tom, is a pious man. I have confidence in his prayers. I have often overheard him pray, when about the barn or stables, and his prayers have always struck me as being quite sincere and earnest. I never heard any foolishness from him. He has always been honest and earnest as a Christian man. Call him.' Tom was called, and came, within the door, dropping his hat and looking tenderly and compassionately at his dying master. The dying man put forth his hand, saying: 'Come, here, Tom. Take my hand. Tom, can you pray for your dying master?' Tom poured out his soul in earnest prayer."

6. The Double Portion produces the utmost devotion to God.

The soul filled with God's Holy Spirit is wholly devoted to Him. Paul was happy to be counted one of the Lord's "slaves." Bishop Taylor counted it joy to turn away from ease and comfort and face danger and hardship anywhere for God. Dr. Keen for love of God and souls brought himself perhaps to a premature grave, and God has had His saints in all ages who have denied themselves, sacrificed themselves, and given themselves whole-souled and exclusively to God and His cause.

7. Produces the best results.

The soul filled with the Spirit of God is more fruitful, more successful, more prosperous, as a consequence. This is particularly true concerning the ministry. Let the preacher receive the baptism of the Spirit, and at once the results of his labours become more abundant and more blessed. " Where the Spirit of the Lord is, there is liberty." So where the Spirit of the Lord is, there is power and where power is there are results well pleasing to God.

A prominent Bishop some years ago said: " If need be, I would stop every item of machinery in the Church, our colleges, seminaries and printing presses; yes, I would stop all our missionaries in the field, all our bishops, editors, pastors, teachers and agents, everything—until we receive the baptism of the Holy Spirit."

It is fire that we need! The fire of the Holy Ghost baptism. The Salvation Army in one of their songs sing thus:

> " God of Elijah, hear our cry,
>   Send the fire!
> He'll make us fit to live or die,
>   Send the Fire.
> To burn up every trace of sin,
> To bring the light and glory in,
> The revolution now begin,
>   Send the Fire! "

> " Thou Christ of burning, cleansing flame,
>   Send the fire!

Thy blood-bought gift today we claim,
Send the fire!
Look down and see this waiting host;
Send us the promised Holy Ghost,
We want another Pentecost.
Send the fire!"

HOW TO OBTAIN THE DOUBLE PORTION

Perhaps we cannot answer that question better than by quoting once again from Dr. Daniel Steele. In the following testimony he tells how the Spirit fell on him and how he received the Double Portion:

"I was led to seek the conscious and joyful presence of the Comforter in my heart. Having settled the question that this was not merely an apostolic blessing, but for all ages, 'he shall abide with you forever,' I took the promise, 'Verily, verily, I say unto you, whatsoever ye shall ask the Father in My name, He will give it you.' The 'verily' had to me all the strength of an oath. Out of the 'whatsoever' I took all temporal blessings, not because I did not believe them to be included, but because I was not then seeking them. I then wrote my own name in the promise, not to exclude others, but to be sure that I included myself. Then writing underneath these words, 'Today is the day of salvation,' I found that my faith had three points to master: the Comforter—for me —now. Upon the promise I ventured with an act of appropriating faith, claiming the Comforter as my right, in the name of Jesus. For several hours I clung by naked faith, praying and repeating Charles Wesley's,

> " ' Jesus, Thine all-victorious love
> Shed in *my* heart abroad.'

" I then ran over in my mind the great facts in Christ's life, especially dwelling upon Gethsemane and Calvary, His ascension, priesthood, and all-atoning sacrifice. Suddenly I became conscious of a mysterious power exerting itself upon my sensibilities. My physical sensations, though not of a nervous temperament, in good health, alone and calm, were like those of electric sparks passing through my bosom with slight painless shocks, melting my hard heart into a fiery stream of love. Christ became so unspeakably precious that I instantly dropped all earthly good,—reputation, property, friends, family, everything—in the twinkling of an eye. My soul crying out:

> " None but Christ to me be given.
> None but Christ in earth or heaven.' "

VII

"DEEPER YET!"

Mrs. Edwards, wife of President Edwards, sought and obtained what she called " the full assurance of faith," and what Methodists call " perfect love," or " holiness," and then gives her glowing experience in the following language: " I cannot find language to express how certain the everlasting love of God appeared; the everlasting mountains and hills were but shadows to it. My safety and happiness, and eternal enjoyment of God's immutable love seemed as durable and unchangeable as God Himself. . . . My soul remained in a heavenly elysium. It was a pure delight which fed and satisfied my soul."

WHEN I was up on the battlefields of France and my regiment was going in towards the front I had some experiences in the dugouts on the St. Mihiel and Argonne fronts. We did not have to make those dugouts, however,—the Germans did that,—and all we had to do was to occupy them as we came up to them. Some of those dugouts were great affairs, deep and immense. When I got down into one of them when night came on I felt almost as comfortable as one could feel out in the S. O. S. No matter how much we may be shelled during the night or how heavy the shells might be that the enemy put across they could hardly penetrate those great German dugouts constructed as they were of iron and cement and built with the idea of standing the heaviest artillery attacks.   Now, often in those dugouts the Lord would preach to me from the text found in Jer. 49: 30, " Dwell deep."   Many a time was a sermon preached to me on *dwelling deep in God,* and I find in these days as I go through the land preaching in the camp-meetings the great need of a deeper work among God's people.   In many places things are very superficial, there is no depth of devotion or piety.   There has been much reliance upon organisation, plans, etc., (and much dependence on great preaching) ; there is not sufficient humility of soul, that clinging to God, that fervency of spirit, that glowing love, that urgency of prayer, that deepness of piety which ought to characterise the people of God.

We stand in need of going deeper yet!   I do not wish now to cast any reflection on the work of God already done in the soul in pardon and purity and holiness.   We must continually praise God for these things, but I am constrained to believe that many forget that the holy life is a progressive life and that if we do not progress in holiness we shall retrograde and drop back into formality, into a dry profession and into a stale experience.   We need to have more experiences such as Evan Roberts, of the Wales Revival, had. He says:

"For a long time I was much troubled in my soul by thinking of the failures of Christianity. Oh! it seemed such a failure—such a failure—and I prayed and prayed, but nothing seemed to give me any relief. But one night, after I had been in great distress praying about this, I went to sleep, and at one o'clock in the morning suddenly I was waked up out of my sleep and I found myself with unspeakable awe, in the very presence of God. And for the space of four hours I was privileged to speak face to face with Him as a man speaks face to face with a friend. At five o'clock it seemed to me as if I had returned to earth again. And it was not only that morning, but every morning for three or four months. Always I enjoyed four hours of that wonderful communion with God. I cannot describe it. I felt it and it seemed to change my whole nature, and I saw things in a different light, and I knew that God was going to work in the land, and not this land only, but the whole world."

The holy Bramwell of early Methodism, who seemed always going farther up into the delectable mountains of God, wrote once these words: "Justification is great, to be cleansed is great; but what is justified or the being cleansed when compared with this being taken into Himself? The world, the noise of self, all is gone; and the mind bears the full stamp of God's image. Here you talk and walk and live, doing all in Him and to Him. Continual prayer and burning all into Christ, in every house, in every company, all things by Him, from Him, and to Him. If things grow slack, Satan suggests 'Nothing can be done.' I answer, much may be done! Plowing, sowing, weeding, pruning may be done; and these will give us hope of a blessed harvest. Go on, do all in love; but go on; never grow weary in well doing."

I carry with me in my travels an old John Wesley hymn book which I ever and anon read with prayerful delight. (In our present hymnal some of Wesley's best hymns are omitted, I am sorry to say.) Let us listen whilst Charles Wesley sings:

> " Now then, my God, thou hast my soul
>   No longer mine, but thine I am;
> Guard thou thine own, possess it whole,
>   Cheer it with hope, with love inflame;
> Thou hast my spirit, there display
>   Thy glory to the perfect day."

John Wesley, at one time, was requested to give his testimony or experience up to the present moment. It is well known that Wesley was very laconic; he was short and terse and crisp. This was the testimony he gave:

> " Jesus, confirm my heart's desire,
>   To work and speak and think for Thee;
> Still let me guard the holy fire
>   And still stir up Thy gift in me.

" Ready for all Thy perfect will,
   My acts of faith and love repeat,
Till death Thy endless mercies seal,
   And make the sacrifice complete."

Again we hear Charles Wesley break out in ardent desire:

" Eager for Thee I ask and pant,
   So strong the principle divine,
Carries me out with sweet constraint
   Till all my hallowed soul is Thine,
Plunged in the Godhead's deepest sea,
   And lost in Thine immensity.

" Come then, my God, mark out Thine heir,
   Of heaven a deeper earnest give;
With clearer light Thy witness bear,
   More sensibly within me live;
Let all my powers Thine entrance feel,
   And deeper stamp Thyself the seal.

" Thee let me drink, and thirst no more
   For drops of finite happiness;
Spring up, O well, in heavenly power,
   In streams of pure perennial peace;
In joy that none can take away,
   In life which shall forever stay."

We are in a time and age when the tendency is towards the unreal, the transitory, the superficial, and we are alarmed at the growing superficiality of the religious and so-called spiritual people. Many are resting in past experiences. They seldom testify to some new experiences and developments in the spiritual realm. Many are effervescent,—

they can shout and cry, and carry on, but there
is no depth of spiritual life and power, and their
prayer life is very deficient. I feel what we want
all along the line is a breaking up before the Lord
—a humbling of ourselves.

That great evangelist, Charles G. Finney, used
to say that he needed frequent breakings up in his
soul—if he went very long without it he would go
dry; he said: " Unless I had the spirit of prayer I
could do nothing. If even for a day I lost the
spirit of grace and supplication, I found myself
unable to preach with power and efficiency or to
win souls by personal conversations. I found myself so borne down with the weight of immortal
souls that I was constrained to pray without ceas-
ing. I cannot tell how absurd unbelief seemed to
me and how certain it was in my mind that God
would answer prayer—those prayers that from day
to day and hour to hour I found myself offering in
such agony and faith. My impression was that the
answer was near, even at the door."

An eminent writer of long ago asks, " What is
the remedy for this fitful, periodic piety, this dis-
graceful alternation of revival and declension, of
foaming fulness and fitful dribble of August
drought? Did God decree that His people should
run low like summer brooks, and is this the normal
condition of the Church which Christ redeemed
unto Himself? Is there not a divine fulness which
can keep a believer always full to the brim, and

can make the Church as steady in its flow as the majestic currents of Niagara?"

Now it must be admitted that we have in our days a good deal of " foaming fulness and fitful dribble of August drought," and I have found some of it right in among our holiness people. We need to recognize it, not deny it, where it exists, and then proceed against it by striking new wells of water and tapping anew the boundless resources of grace. We need to be on the stretch for the " deeper yet " blessing; deeper into love, power, unction and the deeper things of God.

A very devout writer on the deeper life has set forth the following symptoms of a declining state of spirituality. It might be profitable to test out our experience at times by recollecting them. They are as follows:

1. When you grow bolder with sin, or with temptations to sin than you were in your more watchful state—then be sure something is wrong.

2. When you make a small matter of those sins and infirmities which once seemed grievous to you and almost intolerable.

3. When you settle down to a course of religion that gives you but little labour, and leave out the hard and costly part.

4. When your God and Saviour grows a little strange to you, and your religion consists in conversing with *men* and *their books* and not with *God* and *His Book*.

5. When you delight more in hearing and talking, than in secret prayer and the Word.

6. When you use the means of grace more as a matter of duty, than as food in which your soul delights.

7. When you regard too much the eye of man, and too little the eye of God.

8. When you grow hot and eager about some disputed point, or in forwarding the interests of some party of Christians, more than about those matters which concern the great cause of Christ.

9. When you grow harsh and bitter towards those who differ from you, instead of feeling tenderly towards all who love Christ.

10. When you make light of preparing for the Lord's Day, and the Lord's Table, and think more of outward ordinances than you do of heart work.

11. When the hopes of heaven and the love of God do not interest you, but you are thirsting after some worldly enjoyment and grow eager for it.

12. When the world grows sweeter to you and death and eternity are distasteful subjects.

In Madame Guyon's life she tells us of a point in her experience where she lost all "created supports" and fell into "the pure divine." She writes thus: "When I had lost all created supports, and even divine ones, I then found myself happily compelled to fall into the pure divine, and to fall into it through all those very things which seemed

to remove me farther from it. In losing all the
gifts with all its supports I found the Giver. In
losing the sense and perception of Thee in myself,
I found Thee, O my God, to lose Thee no more in
Thyself, in Thine own immutability. O poor
creatures, who pass all your time in feeding upon
the gifts of God and think therein to be the most
favoured and happy, how I pity you if you stop
here short of the true rest and cease to go forward
to God Himself."

Madame Guyon here touches on that aspect of
Christian experience of which Wesley sings:

> " Thy gifts alone will not suffice,
>   O let Thyself be given;
>   Thy presence makes my Paradise,
>   And where Thou art is Heaven."

One has said, " There is a spectacle grander than
the sky, it is the interior of the soul." Yes, truly,
when that soul is washed and made white through
the precious blood! In Songs of Solomon Christ
is represented as saying to the Church, " Thou
art all fair, my love; there is no spot in thee."
Justification rids us of guilt. Regeneration gives
us a new nature, holiness restores the divine
image in the soul and makes the soul all fair—
without spot.

The obtainment of the blessing of holiness is by
faith, but its perfecting and maturing is a matter
of growth. John Wesley wrote to Adam Clark:

" Last week I had an excellent letter from Mrs. Pawson, a glorious witness of full salvation, showing how impossible it is to retain pure love without growing therein."

After a soul is made perfect in love, growth in holiness becomes then much more natural and steady and progressive for the following reasons as stated by John A. Wood:

1. Because all the internal antagonisms of growth are excluded from the heart.

2. Because the purified heart has stronger faith, clearer light, is nearer the fountain and dwells in a purer atmosphere than before it was cleansed.

3. Because after the Holy Ghost has cleansed the heart He has a better chance than before to enlighten, enrich, adorn and renew it, with more and more of love and power.

4. Because the death of sin gives free scope to the life of righteousness.

5. Because the powers and capacities of the entirely sanctified soul increase and expand more rapidly than before.

6. Because holiness is spiritual health. The very conditions of retaining purity are the precise conditions of the most rapid growth.

Fletcher says: " A perfect Christian grows far more than a feeble believer whose growth is still obstructed by the shady thorns of sin and by the draining suckers of iniquity."

Wesley says: "One perfected in love may grow in grace far swifter than he did before."

Bishop Hamline: "The heart may be cleansed from all sin, while our graces are immature, and the cleansing is a preparation for their unembarrassed and rapid growth."

VIII

THE BEAUTY OF HOLINESS

God's Holiness is not so much a particular as a general attribute, it spreads itself over the whole being. Take away holiness from His wisdom, and wisdom would be annihilated, and that would leave cunning. Take away holiness from justice, and you would have cruelty. Take away holiness and you would have false piety; and take it away from truth, and that would leave falsehood. Holiness is His superlative excellence. This is His throne, for " He sits upon the throne of His Holiness." Let us be filled with the Spirit, and then see how we will be separated from sin. Our wisdom, filled with holiness, will be very different from subtlety; our power will have no form of oppression; our sovereignty will be free from tyranny; justice, marked with holiness, will be our mercy, and it will not degenerate into cruelty. You can trace out this thought in its ramifications. You will be elevated into the likeness of God, and pass hither and thither a holy being, and in the religious character there is nothing mean.—ARCHBISHOP TILLOTSON.

"BEAUTY," says Young, "is fair virtue's face, virtue made visible in outward grace." "Beauty," says Michael Angelo, "is the purgation of superfluities." "Supreme beauty," says Winkelmann, "resides in God." Another noted writer speaks of the "Ennobling inspiration springing from the sensibility of the soul toward beauty and sublimity in the natural and moral world." As we contemplate the beauty of holiness we touch those hidden springs of ennobling inspiration.

It has been well said "that all the primary colours in nature coalesce to make pure white." It takes the red, orange, yellow, green, blue, indigo and violet to make a pure white; so the various attributes of holiness join together—coalesce—to produce the pure white light of the beauty of holiness.

If we hold to the figure seven as the number of the primary colours, we may venture to use the same number in enumerating the elements that go to make up the beauty of holiness.

1. The Beauty of Holiness is the beauty of Purity.
2. The Beauty of Holiness is the beauty of Harmony.
3. The Beauty of Holiness is the beauty of Devotion or Consecration.
4. The Beauty of Holiness is the beauty of Humility.
5. The Beauty of Holiness is the beauty of Love.
6. The Beauty of Holiness is the beauty of Christlikeness.
7. The Beauty of Holiness is the beauty of Perfection.

John Fletcher, writing on Christian Perfection, explained it thus:

" We mean nothing but the cluster and maturity of the graces which compose the Christian character in the church militant. In other words, ' Christian Perfection ' is a spiritual constellation made up of those gracious stars—perfect repentance, perfect faith, perfect humility, perfect meekness, perfect self-denial, perfect resignation, perfect hope, perfect charity for our visible enemies as well as for our earthly relation; and above all perfect love for our invisible God through the explicit knowledge of our Mediator, Jesus Christ; and as this last star is always accompanied by all the others, as Jupiter is by his satellites, we frequently use the phrase ' perfect love ' instead of the word perfection, understanding by it the pure love of God shed abroad in the hearts of established believers by the Holy Ghost, which is abundantly given them under the fullness of the Christian dispensation."

Some writers, like Madam Guyon, of the Roman Catholic Church, wrote strongly, truly and beautifully on the subject of sanctification. A long time since, there came to us a very remarkable and beautiful setting of this subject by a Catholic writer. The article is not at hand as we write, but the following notes made from it are very suggestive:

What is sanctified grace? The greatest treas-

ure with which the soul can be enriched—a
treasure in comparison with which all else is value-
less. It is that grace by which the soul comes into
possession of faith like Abraham, patience like
Job, hope like Moses, perseverance like Noah,
meekness like David, temperance like Daniel, prayerfulness like Elijah, unworldliness like James,
boldness like Peter, love like John, guilelessness
like Nathanael, devotion to God and to Jesus like
Paul. It is that grace which will let you sing in
trial like Paul and Silas, help you to pray out of
prison like Peter, keep you in the hottest fire of
affliction like the three Hebrew children. Sanctification is supernatural grace because it takes supernatural power to arrest, to control, to destroy.
Sanctification is an habitual grace. Holiness becomes a habit on earth; here the saints do on earth
as they do in Heaven.

Sanctifying grace imparts sovereign and moral
beauty to the soul so that according to Thomas
Aquinas, that which is in God substantially by His
essence is accidently in the soul by divine participation. It is such beauty God Himself is cap-
tivated with it. " Thou art all beautiful; there is
no spot in thee." It reflects the beauty of the face
of God. Oh, the face of God! Did you ever see
a soul lit up by divine glory? That is but the reflection of the glory of God in the face of Jesus
Christ.

Sanctification is a participation of the divine

nature, a seed of divinity. " His seed remaineth in him." It partakes of the divine nature in the sense the iron partakes of the fire; the rough, rude iron put into the fire becomes radiant, brilliant and the fire may say to it: " I have imparted that to thee." So God may say to the soul, " I impart to thee the glow and beauty and heat of my nature—the soul is bathed in God."

Sanctifying grace assures eternal salvation, conditioned of course upon its continuance in the soul by a living faith and obedience. Possessed with this no soul can be lost.

Sanctifying grace is susceptible of constant increase, and like other riches can be added onto. This is increased by divine bestowments, also by fuller acquirements by exercise and practice. Sanctifying grace gives cause for God's complacency with His saints. God delights in His saints and takes pleasure in them. Sanctifying grace is that by which the soul enjoys God, abounds in His love and becomes more and more like Him—like Him in love, in humility, in sinlessness, in purity, in holiness—" We shall be like Him."

And now, in closing, let us add that sanctification, though instantaneously obtained, is ever capable of improvement, development and progression. As we began with Fletcher so shall we conclude with him by giving some rare words of his concerning growth in holiness and the fullness of

God. Said he: " Filled with all the fullness of
God describes a state of grace infinitesimally
beyond entire sanctification. We enter the sanctified experience from the negative hemisphere, real-
ising the utter elimination of the sin principle
through the cleansing blood. Having passed the
sin side of the experience, we enter the glorious
hemisphere of incoming and abounding grace
which is illimitable in this life and superseded by
the glory of Heaven, sweeps on in a geometrical
ratio through all eternity, ever and anon flooding
the soul with fruitions, amplifications, beautifica-
tions, and rhapsodies eclipsing the most ecstatic
hyperboles, while ages and cycles wheel their
precipitate flight."

Jeremy Taylor wrote: " There is a sort of God's
dear servants who walk in perfectness; and they
have a degree of love and divine knowledge more
than one can discourse of and more certain than
the demonstration of geometry—brighter than the
sun. As the flame touches a flame and combines
into splendour and glory, so is the spirit of a man
united into Christ by the spirit of Christ."

Perhaps there was no man of modern times that
exemplified these things and manifested the beauty
of holiness as did John Fletcher, of early Methodist times. " For seraphic piety, for sanctity that
had no perceptible spot or flaw, he stood alone."
Wesley says: " I was intimately acquainted with
him more than thirty years. During a journey of

many hundred miles I conversed with him morning, noon and night, without the least reserve, and in all that time I never heard him speak an improper word or saw him do an improper action. Many exemplary men have I known, holy in heart and life, within fourscore years, but one equal to him I have not known—one so inwardly and outwardly devoted to God. So unblamable a character in every respect I have not found either in Europe or America." Southey says: " Fletcher in any communion would have been a saint." Isaac Taylor says: " He was a saint, as unearthly a being as could tread the earth at all." Robert Hall says: " Fletcher is a seraph who burns with the ardour of Divine Love. Spurning the fetters of mortality, he almost habitually seems to have anticipated the rapture of the beatific vision."

In 1769, Fletcher, at the request of the Countess of Huntingdon, became president of Treveca seminary for educating young men for the ministry. The Countess describes Fletcher thus: " The reader will pardon me if he thinks I exceed; my heart kindles while I write. Here it was that I saw, shall I say, an angel in human flesh. I should not far exceed the truth if I said so. But here I saw a descendant of fallen Adam, so fully raised above the sins of the fall, that though by the body he was tied down to earth, yet was his whole conversation in heaven; yet was his life from day to day hid with Christ in God. Prayer, praise, love

and zeal, all ardent, elevated above what one would
think attainable in this state of frailty, were the
elements in which he continually lived. Language,
arts, sciences, grammar, rhetoric, logic, even divinity itself, as it is called, were all laid aside when he
appeared in the school room among the students.
And they seldom hearkened long before they were
all in tears, and every heart caught the fire from
the flame that burned in his soul."

> There is a faith unmixed with doubt,
>   A love as free from fear;
> A walk with Jesus where is felt
>   His presence always near.
> There is a rest which God bestows,
>   Transcending pardon, peace;
> A lowly, sweet simplicity
>   Where inward conflicts cease.
>
> There is a service God inspired,
>   A zeal that tireless grows:
> A being " crucified with Christ "
>   Where joy unceasing flows.
> There is a being " right with God,"
>   That yields to His commands,
> Unswerving, true fidelity,
>   A loyalty that stands.
>
> There is a meekness free from pride
>   That feels no anger rise
> At slights, or hate, or ridicule,
>   But crosses counts a prize;
> There is a patience that endures
>   Without a fret or care,
> But joyful signs " Thy will be done,"
>   My Lord's sweet grace I share.

There is a purity of heart,
A cleanness of Desire
Wrought by the holy Comforter,
With sanctifying power.
There is a glory that awaits
Each blood-washed soul on high,
When Christ shall come and take His bride
With Him beyond the sky.

—AUTHOR UNKNOWN.

IX

SPIRITUAL EXPERIENCES

*" Shall I ever forget the summer morning in 1886, not
long after that blessed time of spiritual discovery and
strengthening in the knowledge of God, I experienced
indeed a joy unspeakable and full of glory in the sight
of our Lord and life! Walking out alone I fell into
prayer to be conformed in all things to the will of Him
who had redeemed me and drawn me to Himself. As I
proceeded, while heart and mind were kept in perfect
peace and not the slightest enthusiastic disturbance of
judgment was to be suspected, it was yet as if a heaven
was opened around me and the joy of the Lord flowed
in divine effusion over my being. The glory and beauty
of my Saviour's Person, the indescribable reality of His
presence both in me and around me, the absolute all-
sufficiency of His grace and power, the loveliness and
attraction of His perfect will—all shone upon me with
a brightness of which the August sunshine seemed but
a type and a shadow."*—BISHOP MOULE.

RELIGION is something more, something
greater, than a set of rules, a finespun
theory of morals, or a superstition. The
religion of Jesus Christ is a real soul experience.

Archbishop Usher describes a Christian as one
who has a " heart so all-flowing with the love of
God as continually to offer up every thought, word
and work as a spiritual sacrifice acceptable to God
through Christ."

Lady Huntingdon, famous with the early Methodists, had a deep experience of the deeper things of God and at one time gave her testimony in the following words: "My whole heart has not one single grain, this moment, of thirst after approbation. I feel alone with God; He fills the whole void; I have not one wish, one will, one desire, but in Him; He hath set my feet in a large room. I have wondered and stood amazed that God should make a conquest of all within me by love."

Note the words: "A conquest of all within me by love."

One of Wesley's hymns conveys the thought of this deep experience thus:

> "Thee will I love, my joy, my crown;
> Thee will I love, my Lord, my God;
> Thee will I love, beneath Thy frown
> Or smile, Thy scepter or Thy rod.
> What though my flesh and heart decay!
> Thee will I love in endless day!"

Bishop Whatcoat, of holy memory, tells of some wonderful spiritual experiences he went through. In a letter to Mr. Wesley, the Bishop tells how he was "first born of the Spirit." He says:

"On Sept. 3, 1758, being overwhelmed with guilt and fear, as I was reading . . . I came to these words, 'The Spirit itself beareth witness with our spirits that we are the children of God.' As I fixed my eyes upon them, in a moment my darkness was removed, and the Spirit did bear

witness with my spirit that I was a child of God.
In the same instant I was filled with unspeakable
peace and joy in believing; and all fear of death,
judgment and hell vanished away " . . .

Later the Bishop testified thus: " I soon found
that, though I was justified freely, I was not
wholly sanctified. This brought me into a deep
concern, and confirmed my resolution to admit of
no peace, no, nor truce, with the evils which I still
found in my heart. These considerations led me
to consider more attentively the exceeding great
and precious promises whereby we may escape all
the corruption that is in this world, and be made
partakers of the Divine nature. I saw it was the
mere gift of God, and consequently to be received
by faith, and after many sharp and painful conflicts, and many gracious visitations, on March 28,
1761, my spirit was drawn out and engaged in
wrestling with God for about two hours, in a
manner I never knew before. Suddenly I was
stripped of all but love. I was all love and prayer,
and praise. And in this happy state, rejoicing
evermore, and in everything giving thanks, I continued for some years, wanting nothing for soul or
body more than I received from day to day."

The Christian life is not alone a life of spiritual
enjoyments; it has many conflicts and fights with
the enemy of souls, but the believer becomes wise
as to his devices. 2 Cor. 2: 11. That was a wonderful sermon on " The Devil in Dry Places "

which that great Welsh preacher, Christmas Evans, preached, in which he said:

"I see the unclean spirit rising like a winged dragon, circling in the air, and seeking for a resting-place. Casting his fiery glances toward a certain neighbourhood, he spies a young man in the bloom of life and rejoicing in his strength, seated on the front of his cart, going for lime.

"'There he is,' said the old dragon. 'His veins are full of blood, and his bones of marrow. I will throw into his bosom sparks from hell; I will set all his passions on fire; I will lead him from bad to worse, until he shall perpetrate every sin. I will make him a murderer, and his soul shall sink never again to rise, in the lake of fire.'

"By this time I see him descend with a full swoop toward the earth, but, nearing the youth, the dragon heard him sing:

"'Guide me, O Thou great Jehovah!
    Pilgrim through this barren land;
I am weak, but Thou art mighty,
    Hold me with Thy powerful hand.
        Strong Deliverer,
    Be Thou still my strength and shield.'

"'A dry, dry place this,' says the dragon, and away he goes.

"But I see him again, hovering in the air, and casting about for a suitable resting-place. Beneath his eyes is a flowery meadow watered by a crystal stream, and he describes among the kine a maiden about eighteen years of age, picking up here and there a beautiful flower.

" ' There she is,' says Apollyon, intent upon her soul. 'I will poison her thoughts; she shall stray from the paths of virtue; she shall think evil thoughts, and become impure; she shall become a lost creature in the great city, and at last I will cast her down from the precipice into everlasting burnings.'

" Again he took downward flight, but he no sooner heard her sing the following words, with a voice that might have melted the rocks:

" ' Other refuge have I none,
        Hangs my helpless soul on Thee;
    Leave, ah, leave me not alone,
        Still support and comfort me.'

" ' This place is too dry for me,' says the dragon, and off he flies.

" Now he ascends from the meadow, then, like some great balloon, very much enraged, and breathing forth smoke and fire, and threatening ruin and damnation to all created things.

" ' I will have a place to dwell.' he says, ' in spite of decree, covenant, or grace.'

" As he was thus speaking he beheld a woman, ' stricken in years,' busy with her spinning wheel at her cottage door.

" ' Ah, I see,' says the dragon, ' she is ripe for destruction; she shall know the bitterness of the wail which ascends from the burning marl of hell!'

"He forthwith alights on the roof of the cot, where he hears the old woman repeat with a trembling voice, but with heavenly feeling, the words, 'For the mountains shall depart and the hills be removed, but my kindness shall not depart from thee.'

"'This place is too dry for me,' says the dragon, and away he goes again.

"'In yonder cottage lies old William, slowly wasting away. He has borne the heat and the burden, and altogether he has had a hard life of it. He has very little reason to be thankful for the mercies he has received and has not found serving God a very profitable business. I know I can get him to "curse God and die."'

"Thus musing, away he flew to the sick man's bedside; but as he listened he heard these words: 'Though I walk through the valley of the shadow of death, I will fear no evil, for Thou art with me; Thy rod and Thy staff, they comfort me.'

"Mortified and enraged, the dragon took his flight, saying, 'I will return to the place whence I came.'"

The satisfying grace of God is beautifully illustrated by the following story of one of the early Methodist Circuit Riders, who for many years had preached in the Northwestern Territory; after its division into States he found his operations circumscribed to Indiana. Himself and family had subsisted upon the scanty pittance allowed them— barely enough to keep soul and body together. They had borne their poverty and toil without a murmur. The preacher was much beloved, tall, slender, graceful, with a winning countenance, a kindly eye, where flashed the fire of genius, a voice silvery and powerful in speech, sweet as a wind- harp in song. As the country began to settle, a large landholder, much attached to the preacher, knowing his poverty, wishes to make an expression of his grateful regard and affection. Wherefore he presents him with a title-deed of three hundred and twenty acres—a half section of land. The man of God goes upon his way with a glad and humble heart. Thus he has provision made for his own advancing age, and the wants of his rising family. In three months he returns; alighting at the gate, he removes the saddle-bags and begins to fumble in their capacious pockets. As he reaches the door, where stands his friendly host to wel- come him, he draws out the parchment, saying:

"Here, sir, I want to give you back your title-deed."

"What's the matter?" said his friend, sur- prised; "any flaw in it?"

"No."

"Isn't it good land?"

"Good as any in the State."

"Sickly situation?"

"Healthy as any other."

"Do you think I repent my gift?"

"I haven't the slightest reason to doubt your generosity."

"Why don't you keep it then?"

"Well, sir," said the preacher, "you know I am very fond of singing, and there's one hymn in my book, the singing of which is one of the greatest comforts of my life. I have not been able to sing it with my whole heart since I was here. A part of it runs in this way:

> No foot of land do I possess,
> No cottage in this wilderness:
>   A poor wayfaring man,
> I lodge awhile in tents below;
> Or gladly wander to and fro,
>   Till I my Canaan gain.
>
> Nothing on earth I call my own;
> A stranger to the world unknown,
>   I all their goods despise;
> I trample on their whole delight,
> And seek a country out of sight,
>   A country in the skies.
>
> There is my house and portion fair,
> My treasure and my heart are there,
>   And my abiding home;
> For me my elder brethren stay,
> And angels beckon me away,
>   And Jesus bids me come.

"Take your title-deed," he added; "I had rather sing that hymn with a clear conscience than own America."

X

PREACHING THE GOSPEL

The Gospel preacher has the best field for tender, solemn and sublime eloquence. " The most august objects are presented; the most important interests are discussed; the most tender motives are urged; God and angels, the treason of Satan, the creation, ruin, and recovery of a world, the incarnation, death, resurrection, and reign of the Son of God, the day of judgment, a burning universe, an eternity, a heaven and a hell, all pass before the eye. What are the petty dissensions of the states of Greece, or the ambition of Philip? What are the plots and victories of Rome, or the treason of Catiline, compared with this? If the ministers were sufficiently qualified by education, study, and the Holy Ghost, if they felt their subjects as much as Demosthenes and Cicero did, they would be the most eloquent men on earth, and would be so esteemed wherever congenial minds were found."

FATHER TAYLOR, the sailor preacher of Boston in the long ago, was a most wonderful character—unique, original, mighty. Peter Cartwright, speaking of him, told this story: A lady from the West visited the coast and reported when she got back that there were two cataracts in the United States—Niagara and Father Taylor.

The conversion of Father Taylor started under the preaching of Dr. Griffin, of Park St. Church,

Boston. It was consummated under Elijah Hedding, afterwards Bishop Hedding. Describing Dr. Griffin's preaching that night when he was strangely led into the service, he said: "I was walking along Tremont Street and the bell of Park Street Church was tolling. I put in; and, going to the door, I saw the port was full. I up helm, unfurled topsail and made for the gallery; entered safely, doffed cap or pennant and scud under bare poles to the corner pew. There I hove to, and came to anchor. The old man, Dr. Griffin, was just naming his text, which was: 'But he lied unto him.'"

"As he went on and stated item after item—how the devil lied to men and how his imps led them into sin—I said a hearty 'Amen,' for I knew all about it.

"Pretty soon he unfurled the mainsail, raised the topsail, ran up the pennants to the free breeze; and I tell you, the old gospel never sailed more prosperously. The salt spray flew in every direction; but more especially did it run down my cheeks. I was melted. Everyone in the house wept. Satan had to strike sail; his guns were dismounted or spiked; his various light crafts, by which he led sinners captive, were all beached; and the Captain of the Lord's host rode forth conquering and to conquer. I was young then. I said, 'Why can't I preach so? I'll try it.'"

Father Taylor's description of this preaching

service suggests the essential things that go into effective preaching, which, as one has put it, is: "Speech thrilled by the power of a supernatural conviction and persuasion."

The making of a preacher depends much upon the personal religious experience of the man. Think of that prince of preachers, Bishop Hamline. The depth and power of his preaching must be laid to the deep soul experience of the man. It is told how this came to pass as follows:

When Bishop Hamline was in the height of his usefulness, fulfilling all known duty and attentive to the public and private means of grace, he yet became convinced that his devotions were not so fervent and vital as they might be, that he was lacking in full confidence in drawing nigh to God, that his temper was not always in subjection, and that a sense of unfitness and unworthiness hampered him in his ministerial efforts. Once while walking to church with his wife, he stopped short and exclaimed in his distress, " I could prefer strangling and death to such a state," and yet he was popular, preaching to overflowing congregations. At the first opportunity he threw himself down at the altar and implored the full baptism of the Holy Ghost. The hours passed. He renewed the struggle. He could eat little. He prayed much. He was often in his chamber, kneeling in supplication. A new view of full salvation was given to him. He describes it himself:

"While entreating God for a clean heart my mind was led to contemplate 'the image of Christ as the single object of desire—to be Christ-like, to possess 'all the mind that was in' the blessed Saviour; and this became the burden of my earnest prayer."

And the thought occurred to him: Why not take that image, and take it now? He said:

"Give Him your sin and take His purity. Give Him your shame and take His honour. Give Him your helplessness and take His strength. Give Him your misery and take His bliss. Give Him your death and take His life everlasting. Nothing remains but that you take His in exchange. Make haste! Now, just now, He freely offers you all, and urges all upon your instant acceptance." He adds:

"Suddenly I felt as though a hand omnipotent, not of wrath but of love, were laid upon my brow. That hand, as it pressed upon me, moved downward. It wrought within and without, and wherever it moved it seemed to leave the glorious impress of the Saviour's image. For a few minutes the depth of God's love swallowed me up; all its billows rolled over me."

Under this influence he fell to the floor and cried out in joyful emotion that he had found the fullness, and ever afterward while he lived he was a willing witness to the power of God to make of believers a contented, satisfied and joyful people,

and it was the chief burden of his life to lead souls
to the Saviour into whose perfect likeness he had
been transformed.

The power of preaching lies in the conviction
that the Gospel of the Son of God is the most vital
message that human lips can utter. Alas that so
much time of the pulpit is spent on secondary
subjects!

The Gospel Preacher preaches the certainties of
Salvation and does not refrain from preaching the
terrors of the law as well as the promises of grace.

Some years ago Dr. Buckley, writing on the
subject of preaching in the *New York Christian
Advocate,* inserted a letter from a very thoughtful
Methodist writer who said:

"I have listened to nearly all our bishops, to
many of our secretaries, editors, college presidents,
and other men acknowledged to be our strongest
and best. I have absolute confidence in their honesty of purpose, their goodness, their high character. I have gone from their meetings with the
feeling that God had given Methodism the strongest and best men in the world; *but I never went
from their meetings with the feeling that any one
was in danger.* To me it seems like the clearest of
propositions that they act as if they believe in these
teachings in inverse ratio to their intelligence. Get
together five hundred of the men who acknowledge
to be our strongest and best, men who speak to the
largest congregations, and whose words are re-

ceived with the most authority, and let them answer this question: 'How many souls have come to Christ in the past year in response to your appeals?' How many in truth would make this statement: *'When I was a young man souls flocked to God's altar from my appeals, but as I have grown older and wiser, broader in my comprehension and vision, I seldom see any one saved in my meetings.'* To me the only solution is that while they honestly maintain the old standards as a sacred duty, and earnestly endeavour to make themselves believe the old teachings, deep in their hearts they do not believe them. . . . Today Protestantism stands for a code of laws without penalty, for when we crowd the penalty back and out of sight, and ignore it, practically it ceases to be. . . . Possibly we do not need more doctrinal preaching nor more loyal teaching of the standards, only that the leaders should act as if they had some comprehension of the truth they teach. The most earnest appeal I have listened to for years from a minister (excepting revivalists and men generally regarded as cranks) closed with an invitation. After repeating the awful declaration of Christ concerning the wicked, he said: 'I would not needlessly excite nor alarm anyone, nor will I attempt to explain these words, but they certainly mean something, and my mature judgment is that those out of Christ should seek Him at once. If there is one here tonight who desires to begin the new life, will he please come forward and give me his hand?' Think of a man in a burning hotel, the elevators in flames, the corridors thick with smoke, gently knocking at a door and quietly saying: 'The flames and smoke must mean something, and my mature judgment is that you should seriously think of getting a new boarding place,' and, the man still sleeping, he goes on to say: 'But do not be excited nor needlessly alarmed.' . . . To me it is absolutely impossible to conceive of a man so hard-hearted, so intellectually great, so cold-blooded and icy, so utterly lost to all feelings of love and sympathy for his fellows, as to really believe *in his heart* in the eternal damnation of vast numbers into whose faces he is looking and to whom he is talking, and never arouse them to a sense of their danger, or urge them to flee from the wrath to come."

The Christian Minister often has hard tasks, but he holds on till victory comes. The following incident is told of Stephen Olin, one of the shining lights of the New England Methodist Episcopal ministry:

At one point in his ministry he became greatly discouraged, and attempted to leave his work. A significant dream relieved him. He thought he was working with a pick-axe on the top of a basaltic rock. His muscular arm brought down stroke after stroke for hours; but the rock was hardly indented. He said to himself, " It is use-

less; I will pick no more." Suddenly, a stranger
of dignified mien stood by his side, and thus spoke
to him: "You will pick no more?"

"No."

"Were you not set to this task?"

"Yes."

"And why abandon it?"

"My work is vain; I make no impression on
the rock."

Solemnly the stranger replied: "What is that to
you? Your duty is to pick whether the rock yields
or not. Your work is in your own hands; the
result is not. Work on!"

He resumed his task. The first blow was given
with almost superhuman force, and the rock flew
into a thousand pieces. He awoke, returned to his
work, and a great revival followed. From that
day he never had a temptation to give up his
commission.

The Gospel Minister may have many discour-
agements, but his day of rejoicing will come if he
is faithful. The *Christian Herald* relates the following incident:

"Years ago a Missouri country congregation
listened to a sermon by a young preacher who had
walked twenty miles to deliver it. Tired, hungry,
this youth faltered, floundered and failed. The
people were disgusted; they did not know he had
walked the weary miles, and when the service was
over nobody greeted him, nobody offered him food

or shelter, but as he started down the long road with a breaking heart, the coloured janitor asked him to share his humble meal in a nearby shanty.

"Years passed; the halting young exhorter became Bishop Marvin, of world-wide reputation, and after a full generation he once more stood in that spot to dedicate a great country church. The whole community was assembled; it was a tremendous event in their lives. As the Bishop preached he seemed to detach the people from the world and lift them up to the Great White Throne. When the service was ended and people had come to earthly thoughts again, many crowded about with their carriages and offered lavish hospitality, but the Bishop waved them all aside, and called the old coloured janitor, saying, 'When I was here years ago I was none too good for you and I am none too good for you today.' What a day for that white-headed host and hostess in their cabin and their grown-up children who through the generations that are yet to come will recall the story of the Bishop's visit."

Perhaps no poet has better described the Christian preacher than has the English poet, Cowper. He writes thus:

> " His theme divine,
> His office sacred, his credentials clear,
> By him the violated law speaks out
> Its thunders. And by him in strains as sweet
> As angels use, the Gospel whispers peace.

He stablishes the strong, restores the weak,
Reclaims the wanderer, binds the broken **heart**,
And, arm'd himself in panoply complete
Of heavenly temper, furnishes with arms
Bright as his own, and trains, by every rule
Of holy discipline, to glorious war,
The sacramental host of God's elect."

The Christian Minister is an earnest, strong believer. There is no place for doubt and skepticism in the called minister. He believes, therefore he speaks. Dr. Steele tells us how gloriously he was saved from doubt as follows:

" Salvation from doubts that I am now and forever wholly the Lord's. This is the most astonishing triumph of grace over a temperament naturally melancholic—an introspecting, self-anatomising, and self-accusing style of piety, characteristic of my ancestry. Perfect rest from all apprehension of future ill. Salvation from worry is no small thing; especially in the case of one whose views of life are strongly tinged with indigo. I believe that Jesus, who is the Head over all things to His Church, has the program of my best possible future. My only anxiety, moment by moment, is this—Am I now led by the Spirit of God?"

What shall the message of the Gospel Preacher be? We cannot answer this question better than to place here the testimony of Dr. T. Dinsdale Young, of London, England. Dr. Young probably preaches to the largest congregation of any

Methodist preacher in Europe or America, and the striking thing about it is that this greatest of Methodist congregations *come to hear one of the most orthodox and evangelical Methodist preachers in all Methodism.*

Touching his creed or the things he believes and preaches, Dr. Young says:

"I have always held and preached the absolute finality of Holy Scripture as a Divine Revelation. My persuasion ever deepens that if we are halting in our testimony to the absolute inspiration of the Bible we shall fail in our mission as preachers and churches.   Is not much of the failure today attributable to this cause?

"The Deity of our Lord Jesus Christ has always been the central and basal evangelical truth to me.   The stupendous miracle of the Incarnation has more and more had a leading place in my doctrinal life and teaching.   The Virgin Birth I accept as Revelation and as a necessity of reason too. To me it is unimaginable that the God Man should have an ordinary birth.   I have never receded from the doctrine of the Cross which I received in my evangelical youth.   I was trained to believe that the prime function of the pulpit is to answer the question: 'What must I do to be saved?'   The soteriology of the Reformers is my message of salvation today.   The Witness of the Spirit I believe and preach as the privilege of all saved people.

"That Christ can deliver us from all known sin

has been and is again one of my leading doctrines. That He does this by us with perfect love and that this entire sanctification or Christian holiness is received by faith I steadfastly believe and declare. The Second Advent of our Lord and Saviour has been a dear and delightful doctrine to me. I regard it as the very soul of New Testament teaching and of the Old Testament too. This makes my ministry vivid, intense and glad.

" The morality of the Cross is as sublime as its theology. When we believe in the Crucified, Risen, Enthroned, Interceding, Returning Saviour it makes our lives sublime. A religion of perfect love will please God and be affirmed of men.

" I sing with Charles Wesley amid the shades of evening :

> " ' Happy if with my latest breath
> I may but gasp his name,
> Preach him to all, and cry in death,
> Behold, Behold the Lamb! ' "

Bishop Kavanaugh was one of America's greatest Gospel preachers. One day he was walking through the streets of a city, when he met one of its prominent physicians, who offered him a seat in his carriage. The physician was an infidel. After a while the conversation turned upon religion. " I am surprised," said the infidel doctor, " that such an intelligent man as you are should believe such an old fable as that." The bishop made no immediate reply, but sometime afterwards said: "Doctor, suppose that years ago some one had recommended to you a prescription for pulmonary consumption, and given you directions concerning it, and you had procured the prescription and taken it according to order, and had been cured of the terrible disease. Suppose that you had used the prescription in your practice ever since, and had never known it to fail when taken according to directions, what would you say of the man who could not believe in nor would not try your prescription?" "I should say he was a fool," replied the physician. "Twenty-five years ago I tried the power of God's grace. It made a different man of me. All these years I have preached salvation to others, and wherever it has been accepted I have never known it to fail. I have seen it make the proud man humble, the drunken man temperate, the profane man pure in speech, the dishonest, true. The rich and the poor, the learned and the unlearned, the old and the young have been healed of their diseases." "You have caught me fairly, bishop; I have been a fool," said the physician.

XI

THE NEW THEOLOGY AND THE OLD TIME RELIGION

"Bring us back the Amen Corner that has long been
   frozen out,
For nothing scares the devil like a grand old Metho-
   dist shout.
Bring back the faith of the fathers, its spinal columns
   and grip,
In place of the limp, loose, wriggling of a Higher-
   Critic-ship.
Bring back the hot experience, that an angel might
   rehearse,
For that sigh in the swaddling bands of a little
   threadbare verse.

"Bring back the cross as a refuge from Sinai,
   lightning-scarred,
Conversion through deep conviction, and not through
   signing a card.
Bring back a full salvation, the flower of perfect love,
Till the Church is filled with the fragrance of Para-
   dise above.
Bring back for us, Oh Holy Spirit, whatever we have
   lost—
The might, the joy, the abandon, of fiery Pentecost."
                                      —A. J. HOUGH.

WE are in perilous times,—times of unrest.
turmoil, doubt, skepticism, agnosticism,
infidelity, ultra worldliness. The greatest
peril to the Church is the widespread new theology

teachings which are coming in like a flood. President Strong, of Rochester, N. Y., addressed the McCormick Seminary, Chicago, a few years ago on the new theology. In a most scholarly manner he showed the fallacies and failures of this new fad which has almost destroyed the power of our theological seminaries. He said that this new theology was bad metaphysics, bad morals, and bad theology. He showed how it was impossible for a man who accepted this theology to pray and to worship Christ. With his splendid oratory and magnificent scholarship he revealed what many of us have known for a long time: that the new theology leads directly to atheism; that men denied first the authority of the Bible, then the authority of Jesus Christ, and at last, as some of the professors in the universities now do, deny the existence of God.

Some time before he died General Booth uttered this significant prophecy:

" I consider that the chief dangers that confront the coming century will be: Religion without the Holy Ghost, Christianity without Christ, Forgiveness without Regeneration, Morality without God, and Heaven without Hell."

Bishop Hurst, who is eminent as a scholar, linguist, theologian, historian, and teacher, gives us a very clear and explicit setting of the new theology in his book on Rationalism. In defining Rationalism he is setting forth exactly the main errors and teachings of the thing we call the new theology. He says:

" 1. The errors of Rationalism do not consist of applying reason to divine truth, for truth cannot be appropriated if reason is suppressed or violated. Its errors lie in the following:

"(a) Pelagian rejection of the assistance of grace.

"(b) Dependence upon mere intellectuality divorced from rightly ordered affections and the will.

"(c) A rejection or minimising of a supernatural revelation.

"(d) A repudiation more or less complete of authority—biblical or ecclesiastical, or both."

A recent writer, Mr. Weddell, institutes a comparison between the new theology and the old thus:

" 1. The new theology says that the Bible contains the Word of God. The old theology says that the Bible is the Word of God; the Word judging man rather than man judging the Word.

" 2. The new theology says that Jesus Christ is *a* son of God. The old theology says that Jesus Christ is *the* Son of God.

" 3. The new theology says that the birth of Jesus was *natural.* The old theology says that the birth of Jesus was *supernatural.*

" 4. The new theology says that the death of Jesus Christ was *exemplary.* The old theology says that the death of Jesus Christ was *expiatory.*

" 5. The new theology says that the life of Christ is the life He lived *here on earth*. The old theology says that the true life of Christ is the life He is living *for us at the throne,* this side His bodily resurrection.

" 6. The new theology says that character is built up, like Babel, from *beneath*. The old theology says that real lasting character is something that comes down, like the New Jerusalem, from *above*.

" 7. The new theology says that man is the product of *evolution*. The old theology says that man is God's *special creation*.

" 8. The new theology says that man is the unfortunate *victim of environment*. The old theology says that man is an *actual sinner,* and utterly lost.

" 9. The new theology says that man is justified by *works of his own*. The old theology says that man is justified by faith in the atoning *Blood* of Christ.

" 10. The new theology says that the new life and mature Christianity come by natural *development* of the best that is in us. The old theology says that it comes by miraculous *regeneration and sanctification through* the Holy Spirit.

" 11. The new theology lightly says that prophecy and miracles are of *negligible value*. The old theology reverently accepts them as from God and *authenticating* the Word.

" 12. The new theology says we should aim to *adjust the Gospel* to the times, the *zeitgeist.* The old theology says we should seek only to *adjust the times* to the Gospel, God's gracious Message to all times.

" 13. The new theology says that the Gospel was sent to *save the world.* The old theology says that the Gospel was sent to *save souls* out of the world.

" 14. The new theology sets its hope of the future on men's *civilisation.* The old theology sets its hope on *Christ's Kingdom,* spiritually existent today in men's hearts, and actually and gloriously so tomorrow in all the earth.

" Hence we do devoutly pray, ' Thy Kingdom come; Thy will be done on earth as it is in heaven.' "

Well has Dr. Forsyth, of London, England, said in his " Yale Lectures," (Positive Preaching and the Modern Mind) that the new theology might be more appropriately called a " New Metaphysics "—it is less a theology than a " theosophy." It is in a sense that " wizard twilight " Coleridge knew, and in its soft, subdued colours, Paul's doctrine of sin painted in awful and lurid colours, fades into a colourless nothingness, and the dazzling glory of the Christ—His immaculate conception, His deity, His miracle-working work, His authority, His atonement for sin, His resurrection—all are toned down

and sweetly shaded to hide the rugged supernatural, and to shut out of view the unexplainable
mystery of the miraculous.

Touching now the Old Time Religion, we want
to observe some of its chief and triumphant
characteristics.

When George Whitefield was shaking England
with the thunders of his Revival preaching, a certain Baronet said to a friend, Mr. B., " This Whit-
field is truly a great man—he is the founder of a
new religion."

" A new religion!" exclaimed Mr. B.

" Yes," said the baronet. " What do you
call it?"

" Nothing but the old religion revived with energy, and heated as if the minister really meant
what he said," replied Mr. B.

Bishop Ryle, of Liverpool, England, speaking in
his day on the religious situation, said, " Our chief
medicine for the spiritual diseases of the nine-
teenth century is a bold and unhesitating inquiry
for the old paths, old doctrines and the faith of the
days that are past."

(1) The Old Time Religion has been characterised by *deep conviction of Sin.* Peter Bohler,
when trying to lead John Wesley into saving faith,
said of him, " He wept bitterly while I was talking
upon the subject and afterwards asked me to pray
for him. I can freely affirm that he is a poor,
broken-hearted sinner, hungering after the right-

eousness of Christ."   The soul under deep conviction of Sin says:

> Guilty, I stand before Thy face;
> On me, I feel Thy wrath abide;
> 'Tis just, the sentence should take place;
> 'Tis just; but O Thy Son hath died.

(2) The Old Time Religion stands for radical and thorough conversion.

Thomas Walsh was brought up an Irish Catholic, but under the preaching of the East Methodists, got under conviction. "The arrows of the Almighty," he says, "stuck fast in me and my very bones trembled, because of my sins."

Under a sermon on "Who is this that cometh from Edom with dyed garments from Bozrah," he got gloriously converted. "I was divinely assured," he says, "that God for Christ's sake had forgiven me all my sins; the Spirit of God bore witness with my spirit that I was a child of God. I broke with tears of joy and love." He became one of the marvels of early Methodism—a miracle of grace himself, and a mighty preacher of the saving Grace of God.

(3) The Old Time Religion proclaims a full redemption.

In the old Methodist hymn book, a section is devoted to "Seeking for full Redemption," because this was a great truth among the Methodists.

Dr. Daniel Steele was a wonderful example of

this grace. Under the revival, conductd by A. B. Earle, he says: " I went where St. Paul did, when he heard words not lawful to be uttered. Suddenly I became conscious of a mysterious power exerting itself upon my sensibilities. Christ became so unspeakably precious to me, that I instantly dropped all earthly good, reputation, property, friends, family, everything in the twinkling of an eye and my soul cried out:

> " None but Christ to me be given,
> None but Christ in earth or heaven."

It was then that Dr. Steele entered with the life of full redemption which made him to our Church the John Fletcher of our later Methodism.

(4) The Old Time Religion has brought some wonderful revivals of religion.

Those revivals have been characterised by the most extraordinary outpourings of the Spirit of God.

A preacher said: " Whitefield, morning and evening, preached to nearly seven or eight thousand people and God's power was so much amongst us at the afternoon sermon that the cries and groans of the people would have drowned my voice." In one of his meetings it is said that there were thirty thousand present and about ten thousand were converted.

Through its continuous and great revival, Methodism grew in the early days by leaps and bounds. In a little over a quarter of a century, it had grown from 65,000 members to nearly 350,-000. Abel Stevens attributes this growth largely to its revivalistic fervour and passion.

That great preacher of Eastern Methodism, Charles Pitman, was sent to St. George's M. E. church in 1836. In the fall of that year, there were indications of a revival. Pitman came into the church one Sunday night and preached from Psa. 126: 6. As he preached the congregation became rapt in amazement at his wonderful utterances and the people were swayed like the wind sways the growing grain. A wave of heavenly power swept over the people that was indescribable. Scores rushed to the altar crying for mercy and saints shouted the praises of God. Within three months over thirteen hundred souls found the Lord; seven hundred and fifty were added to St. George's church. Oh for some of the old-fashioned revivals to come again to the church, but it is useless to hope for them unless our churches are willing to pay the old time price for them!

(5) The Old Time Religion brings triumphant dying.

A dying saint said "he was going to that country he had all his life wished to see," and just before he died he burst into singing of the things he saw.

How much sweeter to die that way than like the

learned philosopher of one of our colleges—a man who had been a leader in the " religious education " movement of recent years, but who had been a doubter of religious realities—when he was dying he said: " I do not know where I am going." The old time religion is good to live by and glorious in the hour of death.

(6) The Old Time Religion begets a passion for soul saving. John Smith, the mighty soul winner of England, said: " I am a broken-hearted man; not for myself, but on account of others; God has given me such a sight of the value of precious souls that I cannot live if souls are not saved. Give me souls or else I die."

Doddridge said, " I long for the conversion of souls more sensibly than for anything else. Methinks I could not only labour for it but die for it with pleasure."

Whitefield cried out: " I have prayed a thousand times till the sweat has dropped from my face like rain, that God would not let me enter the ministry till He thrust me forth to His work."

Wesley said: " I would throw by all the libraries in the world rather than be guilty of the loss of one soul."

Rankin, of early Methodism, said: " I could lay down my life if I might be instrumental in saving one soul from everlasting ruin."

XII

PERFECT LOVE

To be cleansed from sin is a preparation for growth.
My soul is confidentially engaged with God.
To be alive to God is, as it were, two heavens.
O run the race, fight the battle, conquer through the blood.
I am nearer the throne, and never was so dependent on Jesus.
I sink at Christ's feet and say Glory, Glory!
The world, the noise of self is all gone, and the mind bears the full stamp of God's image.—BRAMWELL.

THE great subject of Full Salvation has been written about and preached under a number of names or terms, such as: " Entire Sanctification," " Christian Perfection," " Full Redemption," " The Fulness of the Blessing," " The Rest of Faith," " Saved to the Uttermost," " Full Assurance of Faith." The early Methodists were wont to use the term " Perfect Love," a great deal. One of the greatest books ever written upon the subject of full salvation is entitled " Perfect Love." This book, by Rev. John A. Wood, has had the widest reading of any holiness book. Unquestionably it sets forth the doctrine of Christian Holiness with a clearness and fulness and sweetness that makes it the best exposition of the doctrine that is to be found in any volume.

I feel convinced that the cause of Christian Holiness has been hurt seriously by so many getting away from the thought that the deep experience of entire sanctification is nothing more or less than Perfect Love.

We have a lot of holiness so-called of the carping, criticising, antagonising, censorious, fire-eating, noisy, rackety, rough and boisterous kind that do little else than alienate a lot of good people from it.

A development and cultivation of the " Perfect Love " type of Christian Holiness, I am persuaded, would do much to further the experience and doctrine among professing Christians.

Let us consider some aspects of " Perfect Love." Listen to Wesley as he sings of it:

> " O glorious hope of Perfect Love!
> It lifts me up to things above,
> It bears on eagles' wings;
> It gives my ravished soul a taste,
> And makes me for some moments feast
> And Jesus' priests and kings."

Wesley defines the experience thus: " The loving God with all our heart, mind, soul and strength; this implies that no wrong temper, none contrary to love remains in the soul and that all the thoughts, words and actions are governed by pure love."

Writing upon the Excellency of Divine Love, Wesley says: "Love is the fulfilling of the law, the end of the commandment." Very excellent things are spoken of love; it is the essence, the spirit, the life of all virtue. It is not only the first and great command, but it is all the commandments in one. Whatsoever things are just, whatsoever things are pure, whatsoever things are amiable, or honourable; if there be any virtue, if there be any praise, they are all comprised in this one word, love. In this is perfection, glory, and happiness; the royal law of heaven and earth is this: "Thou shalt love the Lord thy God with all thy heart, and with all thy soul, and with all thy mind, and with all thy strength."

Lady Huntingdon, famous with the early Methodists, had a deep experience of Perfect Love and at one time gave her testimony in the following words: "My whole heart has not one single grain, this moment, of thirst after approbation. I feel alone with God; He fills the whole void; I have not one wish, one will, one desire but in Him; He hath set my feet in a large room. I have wondered and stood amased that God should make a conquest of all within me by love."

Note the words: "A conquest of all within me by love."

Archbishop Usher describes a Christian as one who has a "heart so all-flowing with the love of God as continually to offer up every thought, word

and work as a spiritual sacrifice acceptable to God
through Christ."

The language of the sanctified soul is:

"Thee will I love, my joy, my crown;
Thee will I love, my Lord, my God;
Thee will I love, beneath Thy frown
Or smile, Thy scepter or Thy rod.
What though my flesh and heart decay!
Thee will I love in endless day!

Mrs. Edwards, wife of President Edwards,
says, "In 1742 I sought and obtained the full
assurance of faith. I can not find language to
express how certain the everlasting love of God
appeared: the everlasting mountains and hills were
but shadows to it. My safety and happiness, and
eternal enjoyment of God's immutable love, seemed
as durable and unchangeable as God Himself.
Melted and overcome by the sweetness of this
assurance, I fell into a great flow of tears, and
could not forbear weeping aloud."

"The presence of God was so near and so real
that I seemed scarcely conscious of anything else.
My soul was filled and overwhelmed with light,
and love, and joy in the Holy Ghost, and seemed
just ready to go away from the body. This exalta-
tion of soul subsided into heavenly calm and a rest
of soul in God, which was even sweeter than what
preceded it."

Perfect Love is another term for the Canaan
experience. Rev. Dr. Payson says, "Were I to

adopt the figurative language of Bunyan, I might
date this letter from the land of Beulah, of which
I have been for some weeks a happy resident.

"The Celestial City is full in my view; its
glories beam upon me; its breezes fan me; its
odours are wafted to me; its sounds strike my ears,
and its spirit is breathed into my heart. Nothing
separates me from it but the river of death, which
now appears but as an insignificant rill, that may
be crossed at a single step whenever God gives
permission.

"The Sun of righteousness has been gradually
drawing nearer and nearer, appearing larger and
brighter as He approached, and now He fills the
whole hemisphere, pouring forth a flood of glory,
in which I seem to float like an insect in the beams
of the sun, exulting, yet almost trembling, while I
gaze upon this excessive brightness, and wonder-
ing, with unutterable wonder, why God should
deign thus to shine upon a simple worm."

After experiencing this great increase of faith,
Dr. Payson cried out, in view of his former
distressing doubts, and the great loss he had
thereby sustained in his own enjoyment and
usefulness, "O that I had known this twenty
years ago!"

When Bishop Whatcoat got the blessing he said,
"My spirit was drawn out and engaged in wrestling with God for about two hours in a manner I
never knew before. Suddenly I was stripped of all

but love. I was all love and prayer and praise, and in everything giving thanks, I continued wanting nothing for soul or body more than I received from day to day." Lady Huntingdon, of early Methodism, says, " I have wondered and stood amazed that God should make a conquest of all within me by love."

A certain writer sets forth the following ten marks of Perfect Love:

1. Easy victory over sin.
2. Oneness with Christ.
3. No apprehension of future ill.
4. Insatiable desire to communicate the love of Christ to unbelievers.
5. Increased beneficence, enlarged liberality.
6. Hunger for the word of God.
7. Duty changed to delight.
8. Humility.
9. Chronic faith.
10. Joy and power.

Perfect Love is an experience which all God's children may enjoy, but alas! so many professing Godliness show no interest in the deep things of God. Others there are whose reasonings and philosophy keep them from attaining the fulness of the blessing.

Among the mighty men of the Philadelphia Conference was Rev. Dr. Hodgson. He was a great preacher and leader of the hosts of the Lord. In a convention of Methodists in Philadelphia, 1840,

Dr. Hodgson read a paper on "The Type of
Piety Necessary to the Highest Prosperity of the
Church," in which he said: "If the inspired writers pray that the people of God may be made and
kept entirely holy in this life; if they declare it to
be the design of God, in the plan of salvation, that
Christians should be thus purified and preserved;
if, in accordance with these facts, entire holiness
is explicitly and peremptorily enjoined by the great
Author of our salvation; if the apostles exhort
Christians to direct efforts to attain to it; if they
propose it as the constant aim of Christians; if
they declare it to be the great object of all their
teaching and other labours; if entire holiness is the
standard to which they sought to conform their
own experience; if divine influences, both necessary and sufficient to place and maintain Christians in that state, are promised; further, if it is
alleged to be a fact in the divine administration
that God does confer the promised grace on those
that seek it; and if examples are recorded in which
it was attained and exemplified, what remains but
that I must accept the doctrine and maintain it?
I love it.   I love those that love it.   And I love
them the more because they love it.   That there
are doctrines connected with it which are not true,
and imperfect expositions of it, and measures employed for its promotion which are open to criti-
cism, and dangers to guard against, I do not deny,
but I AM DETERMINED NOT TO BE THE MERE

WATCHDOG OF ORTHODOXY, BARKING AND HOWL-
ING, AND KEPT BACK BY AN INVISIBLE CHAIN,
WHILE MY BRETHREN, WITH SOME ERRORS, AS I
SUPPOSE, GO INTO THE BANQUETING HOUSE OF THE
GREAT KING, AND SIT DOWN TO THE FEAST OF FAT
THINGS. I INTEND TO GO IN WITH THEM AND
PARTAKE OF THE RICH PROVISION."

Hear further testimonies from those who went
into the king's banqueting house and sat down to
the " feast of fat things " and testify thus:

Rev. Henry Smith, for many years a prominent
preacher in the Baltimore Conference, says:
" After a long and painful struggle, my soul, by
simple believing, stepped into liberty. I am happy,
solidly happy in the enjoyment of perfect love."
The high plane of perfect love is not reached by
any without a hard struggle; but when reached,
the believer is regarded a thousand-fold.

Mrs. Phoebe Palmer, who during her life led
twelve thousand souls to Christ for pardon, and
thousands over into the land of perfect love, in
speaking of the blessing says: " I rejoice in the
assurance that I was wholly sanctified throughout
body, soul and spirit. O, with what triumph did
my soul expatiate on the infinitude of the atonement! I saw its unbounded efficacy as sufficiency
to cleanse a world of sinners, and present them
faultless before the throne. I felt that I was enabled to plunge and lose myself in this ocean of
purity. Yes,

" Plunged in the Godhead's deepest sea,
And lost in love's immensity."

Rev. William Bramwell rejoices in the Lord in the following words: " The Lord, for whom I had waited, came suddenly to the temple of my heart. My soul was all wonder, love and praise." And for twenty-six years he walked in this glorious liberty.

Dr. Upham, one of the noble saints of God on earth, says: " I was distinctly conscious when I reached it. I was redeemed by a mighty power, and filled with the blessing of perfect love."

XIII

IF I LOSE MY FAITH

"Faith is the Christian's right eye," as Thomas Brooks, the Puritan, said, "through which he can see for Christ; faith is the Christian's right hand, by which he can do for Christ; faith is the Christian's tongue, by which he can speak for Christ; faith is the Christian's vital spirit, by which he can act for Christ."

Faith is a principle pertaining to eternity as well as time.

To cherish infidelity is to paralyse one of the noblest faculties of the soul.

THIS age is peculiarly perilous to faith. Unbelief, skepticism and infidelity meet us at every turn. The enemy has come in like a flood and put out the fires of faith and the damps of unbelief fill the air and choke the soul. Like Ezekiel's army of dry bones, we behold multitudes with no breath in them.

There is a famine of faith in the land. We build quarter million, half million and million dollar churches, but faith is not found in them; we organise great concerns but they carry on without faith; we pour out millions in schools and colleges but they fast become slaughter houses of faith and their products canned goods only.

In one of my day dreams I met Faith coming

out of Church; her face was sad, tears were in her eyes. I said: " Faith, why weepest thou? " She said, " I went into my Father's house, I went to the pulpit, but when the preacher saw me he hastily removed me, saying that Reason alone would be allowed to sit with him. I went to the choir, but they put me out, saying that ' Sentiment was all they wanted, not Faith.' I went to the prayer-meeting, but they dismissed me from there, saying that ' Good Works were all they cared for.' I went to the Upper Room, but it had not been swept or garnished for many a month, as no one used it now. I went to the Supper Room, and they bade me be gone, as ' Service took the place of Faith with them.' " " But," I said, " Faith, hast thou not friends in the schools? Why not go there? " Faith answered, " Time was when the professors received me, but not now. I have been turned out of doors by men of learning and the students have mocked me. Intellect and Pride sit now in the chief seats of the schools, and for me there is no place." " But, Faith," again I said, " Why not go to the homes; surely there must be a place for thee there." And Faith replied, " Not so; once the family altar was removed, I was dismissed. Jazz music and songs now take the place of the songs of Zion; newspapers and novels crowd out the Bible; the voice of prayer is no longer heard and mad pleasure takes the place of quiet repose and the fear of God seems no longer known." I said, "Faith, what then is to become of thee?" Faith answered, "I shall remain upon the earth as an outcast among the many; I shall visit the humble and the contrite and the poor in spirit. I shall be as a stranger and a pilgrim till these evil days are past. It is dark now, but the morning will break again; the long, long night shall pass away and the Church will awake from its stupour and shake off the fetters of unbelief and will open its doors again to me and the schools and the homes will welcome me once more."

Leaving my dream and coming to the subject in hand—"If I lose my faith," let me set down a few things that inevitably happen when a man loses his faith.

1. If I lose my faith I lose my Bible. The Bible continues no longer to be the word of the Lord. It becomes a bit of literature only made up of myth, folk-lore, patchwork, etc. It is no longer an inspired book and therefore fails to inspire me. Its inspiration is no more than the inspiration of poets or sages or philosophies of ancient days or modern times. I no longer read it with reverence nor hear it speak from its depths to the deepest needs of my soul.

2. If I lose my faith I lose my God and Saviour. Wesley sang:

> "Spirit of Faith come down,
> Reveal the things of God,

And make to me the Godhead known
And witness with the blood."

When I lose my faith God becomes obscured to
me and my Saviour's face is hidden and His voice
I hear no more.   God becomes an unknown Power
and a Force in nature and Christ becomes a strange
figure of history—unique and wonderful as a man,
as a teacher, hero and martyr.   He is no longer
my "Redeemer from all Sin," "The Rose of
Sharon and the Lily of the Valley."   No more is
he the Captain of my salvation and the Lamb of
God taking away my sin.

3. If I lose my faith I lose the assurance of my
salvation and the forgiveness of my sins.   I shall
sing no longer,

"Happy day, happy day,
When Jesus washed my sins away."

Nor can I sing:

"Blessed assurance, Jesus is mine;
Oh what a foretaste of glory divine."

Sin and sins, like dark heavy clouds, obscure
my skies and the Sun of Righteousness no longer
shines with healing in its wings in my soul.
Doubt takes the place of assurance, darkness the
place of light, fears and forebodings possess my
soul and there is no peace and no holy quiet as in
other days.

4. If I lose my faith I lose my hymn book.
Dear to me next to my Bible is the old hymn book.
With my faith gone the old hymns are meaning-
less—so much poetry only. I can no longer sing:

> " My God I am thine,
>   What a comfort divine,
>   What a blessing to know
>   That Jesus is mine."

> " Peace, doubting heart! My God's I am.
>   Who formed me man, forbids me fear;
>   The Lord hath called me by my name,
>   The Lord protects, forever near;
>   His blood for me did once atone,
>   And still He loves and guards His own."

> " My God is reconciled,
>   His pardoning voice I hear;
>   He owns me for His child,
>   I can no longer fear.
>   With confidence I now draw nigh,
>   And Father, Abba Father, cry!"

5. If I lose my faith I lose Prayer and Communion with God.

> " Prayer is the soul's sincere desire,
>   Uttered or unexpressed,
>   The motion of a hidden fire
>   That trembles in the breast."

In prayer my soul draws near to God in the
hour of need and He meets me and hears and answers. " Heaven comes down my soul to greet,
and glory crowns the mercy seat." Prayer is more

than asking; it is also communion with God. Such
was it to Moses on the Mount when he spake face
to face with God as a friend speaks to a friend,
and the glory settled on Moses' face and the skin
of his face shone when he came down to Aaron
and the tribes. Now if I lose my faith prayer becomes to me of no avail, because, " he that cometh
to God must believe that He is, and that He is a
rewarder of them that diligently seek him."

6. If I lose my faith the Christian Religion becomes only one of many religions and a part of a
big cosmic process. When faith dies out religion
is viewed as an intuitive something common to the
race and may be dispensed with when man arrives
at that place of proud superior (?) intellect where
himself becomes a god, the architect of his own
soul and the captain of his fate.

7. If I lose my faith the great doctrines of grace
are replaced by those of modern times and the
faith of the fathers becomes the object of aversion
and attack. The doctrine of the blood of Jesus
atoning for sinners becomes a thing of distaste and
repudiation; the doctrine of Sin and Depravity
becomes the object of ridicule and scorn; the doctrine of Repentance becomes unnecessary; the
doctrine of Regeneration is supplanted by Reformation, Salvation by Education and Culture.
Progression stamps out sanctification. The doctrine of the Divine about Christ must be " according to the best scientific and philosophical methods

education can give us . . . to use the language
of the schools, Christ functions in our life as
God. . . . His cross is the summary of God's
method in social evolution, in the progress of justice, in the hope of human betterment." (Shailer
Matthews.)

In short, to lose my faith is to take my soul out
of the hands of the Divine Christ, wrest it from
the faith once delivered unto the saints, and com-
mit it into the hands of higher critics and wander
on in doubt and dismay and darkness here, and
finally make my bed in hell.

8. If I lose my faith I have no gospel to preach.
Paul declared the gospel to be the "power of God
unto salvation to every one that believeth." If I
lose faith in the old gospel I have nothing to preach
but human opinions, questionable philosophy. and
the uncertain findings of the critics. The pulpit
becomes no longer a theme of power, but a reading
desk; the prophet is silent and the guesser takes
his place. The herald of a great salvation becomes
a harker of second-hand clothes worn by Kant,
Ritschl, Welhausen, Strauss, Renan, etc.

Finally, if I lose my faith I lose the Preaching
Passion. A higher critic in the pulpit knows
nothing of the fire of the Holy Ghost; a minister
of doubting skeptical turn of mind never preaches
with passion; unbelief and doubt put out the fires
of the soul. "We are living," says a recent
writer, "in an age which robs religion of its in-

flammatory touch. We have enthroned the intellect and dethroned passion. It is an inexcusable thing for a herald of God to lack earnestness . . . only the bleeding heart can bless."

Printed in the United States of America

www.ingramcontent.com/pod-product-compliance
Lightning Source LLC
Chambersburg PA
CBHW020949030426
42339CB00004B/14